OCR SHP GCSE

THE ELIZABETHANS
1580–1603

JAMIE BYROM
MICHAEL RILEY

The Schools History Project

Set up in 1972 to bring new life to history for school students, the Schools History Project has been based at Leeds Trinity University since 1978. SHP continues to play an innovatory role in history education based on its six principles:

- Making history meaningful for young people
- Engaging in historical enquiry
- Developing broad and deep knowledge
- Studying the historic environment
- Promoting diversity and inclusion
- Supporting rigorous and enjoyable learning

These principles are embedded in the resources which SHP produces in partnership with Hodder Education to support history at Key Stage 3, GCSE (SHP OCR B) and A level. The Schools History Project contributes to national debate about school history. It strives to challenge, support and inspire teachers through its published resources, conferences and website: http://www.schoolshistoryproject.co.uk

This resource is endorsed by OCR for use with specification OCR Level 1/2 GCSE (9-1) in History B (Schools History Project) (J411). In order to gain OCR endorsement, this resource has undergone an independent quality check. Any references to assessment and/or assessment preparation are the publisher's interpretation of the specification requirements and are not endorsed by OCR. OCR recommends that a range of teaching and learning resources are used in preparing learners for assessment. OCR has not paid for the production of this resource, nor does OCR receive any royalties from its sale. For more information about the endorsement process, please visit the OCR website, www.ocr.org.uk.

The publishers thank OCR for permission to use specimen exam questions on pages 104 and 105 from OCR's GCSE (9-1) History B (Schools History Project) © OCR 2016. OCR have neither seen nor commented upon any model answers or exam guidance related to these questions.

Note: The wording and sentence structure of some written sources has been adapted and simplified to make them accessible to all pupils while faithfully preserving the sense of the original.

Every effort has been made to trace all copyright holders, but if any have been inadvertently overlooked, the Publishers will be pleased to make the necessary arrangements at the first opportunity.

Although every effort has been made to ensure that website addresses are correct at time of going to press, Hodder Education cannot be held responsible for the content of any website mentioned in this book. It is sometimes possible to find a relocated web page by typing in the address of the home page for a website in the URL window of your browser.

Hachette UK's policy is to use papers that are natural, renewable and recyclable products and made from wood grown in well-managed forests and other controlled sources. The logging and manufacturing processes are expected to conform to the environmental regulations of the country of origin.

Orders: please contact Hachette UK Distribution, Hely Hutchinson Centre, Milton Road, Didcot, Oxfordshire, OX11 7HH. Telephone: +44 (0)1235 827827. Email education@hachette.co.uk Lines are open from 9 a.m. to 5 p.m., Monday to Friday. You can also order through our website: www.hoddereducation.co.uk

ISBN: 978 1 4718 6098 0

© Jamie Byrom, Michael Riley 2016

First published in 2016 by
Hodder Education,
An Hachette UK Company
Carmelite House
50 Victoria Embankment
London EC4Y 0DZ

www.hoddereducation.co.uk

The authorised representative in the EEA is Hachette Ireland, 8 Castlecourt Centre, Dublin 15, D15 XTP3, Ireland (email: info@hbgi.ie)

Impression number   10 9 8
Year   2024

All rights reserved. Apart from any use permitted under UK copyright law, no part of this publication may be reproduced or transmitted in any form or by any means, electronic or mechanical, including photocopying and recording, or held within any information storage and retrieval system, without permission in writing from the publisher or under licence from the Copyright Licensing Agency Limited. Further details of such licences (for reprographic reproduction) may be obtained from the Copyright Licensing Agency Limited, www.cla.co.uk.

Cover photo: DeAgostini/Getty Images

Typeset by White-Thomson Publishing Ltd

Printed and bound by CPI Group (UK) Ltd, Croydon CR0 4YY

A catalogue record for this title is available from the British Library.

CONTENTS

	Introduction **Making the most of this book**	2
1	Majesty **How did Elizabeth use her power?** *Closer look 1* – Elizabeth in film and on television	8
2	'Dangerous people' **Why were there so few Catholics in Elizabeth's kingdom by 1603?** *Closer look 2* – 'Little John' and how he is remembered	26
3	Daily lives **What mattered to the Elizabethans?** *Closer look 3* – Inside Montacute House	44
4	Merry England? **What lay behind changes in popular culture?** *Closer look 4* – May Day and the myth of 'Merry England'	62
5	Going global **What did the Elizabethan adventurers achieve?** *Closer look 5* – Dead and *not* gone	80
	Preparing for the examination	98
	Glossary	106
	Index	108
	Acknowledgements	110

Introduction

Making the most of this book

● Where this book fits into your GCSE history course

The course

The GCSE history course you are following is made up of five different studies. These are shown in the table below. For each type of study you will follow **one** option. We have highlighted the option that this particular book helps you with.

OCR SHP GCSE B
(Choose one option from each section)

Paper 1 1 ¾ hours	**British thematic study** ● The People's Health ● Crime and Punishment ● Migrants to Britain	20%
	British depth study ● The Norman Conquest ● The Elizabethans  ● Britain in Peace and War	20%
Paper 2 1 hour	**History around us** ● Any site that meets the given criteria.	20%
Paper 3 1 ¾ hours	**World period study** ● Viking Expansion ● The Mughal Empire ● The Making of America	20%
	World depth study ● The First Crusade ● The Aztecs and the Spanish Conquest ● Living under Nazi Rule	20%

The British depth study

The British depth study focuses on a short time span when the nation was under severe pressure and faced the possibility or actual experience of invasion. The point of this study is to understand the complexity of society and the interplay of different forces within it. You will also learn how and why historians and others have interpreted the same events and developments in different ways.

Introduction

As the table shows, you will be examined on your knowledge and understanding of the British depth study as part of Paper 1. You can find out more about that on pages 98 to 105 at the back of the book.

Here is exactly what the specification shows for this depth study.

The Elizabethans, 1580–1603

The specification divides this period study into five sections:

Sections and issues	Learners should study the following content:
Elizabeth and government Issue: the power of the Queen	• Elizabeth and her court including the Privy Council and the rebellion of the Earl of Essex • Elizabeth and her parliaments including opposition from Puritans • Elizabeth and her people including local government and propaganda
Catholics Issue: the nature and extent of a Catholic threat	• The enforcement of Elizabeth's religious settlement after 1580 • Catholic links abroad, plots against Elizabeth, and the Elizabethan spy network • Mary Queen of Scots, the Armada and war with Spain
Daily lives Issue: the nature and dynamics of Elizabethan society	• The contrasting lives of rich, middling and poor Elizabethans • Family life: husbands and wives, parents and children, wider kinship • Poverty: its causes, Elizabethan explanations and responses
Popular culture Issue: 'Merry England'	• Theatres and their opponents • The Puritan attack on popular culture • The persecution of witches
The wider world Issue: the significance of England's connections with the wider world	• Imperial ambition: the motives and achievements of Elizabethan adventurers • Roanoke: England's attempt at an American colony • Trade with Asia, including first contacts with India

You need to understand the interplay between these forces in society:

- Political
- Religious
- Economic
- Social
- Cultural

You need to pay special attention to this underlying issue:

How and why late Elizabethan England has been interpreted as a 'golden age' and the reasons why this interpretation has been challenged.

You should study a range of types of interpretation including:

- academic (historians)
- educational
- popular (e.g. television)
- fictional.

The next two pages show how this book works.

How this book works

The rest of this book (from pages 8 to 97) is carefully arranged to match what the specification requires. It does this through the following features:

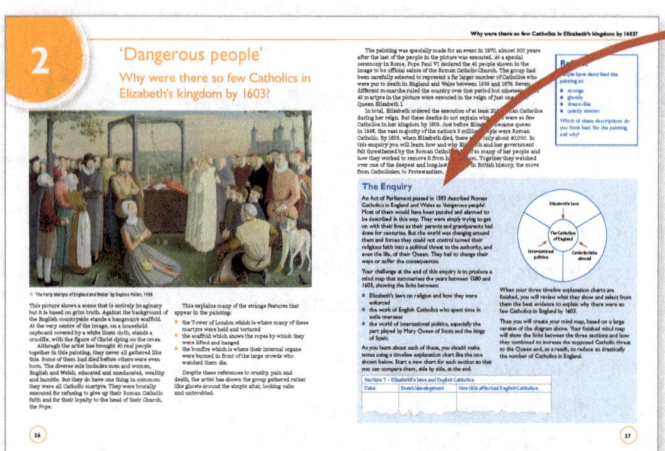

Enquiries

The book is largely taken up with four 'enquiries'. Each enquiry sets you a challenge in the form of an overarching question.

The first two pages of the enquiry set up the challenge and give you a clear sense of what you will need to do to work out your answer to the main question. You will find the instructions set out in 'The Enquiry' box, on a blue background, as in this example.

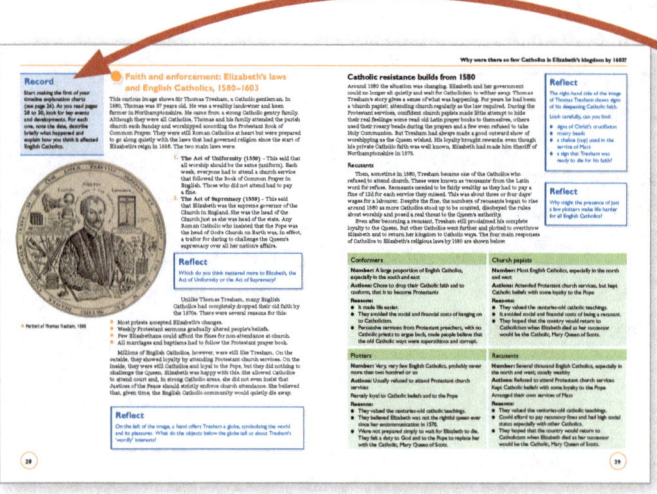

Record tasks

From that point, the enquiry is divided into three sections. These match the bullet points shown in the specification on page 3. You can tell when you are starting a new section as it will start with a large coloured heading like the one shown here. Throughout each section there are 'Record' tasks, where you will be asked to record ideas and information that will help you make up your mind about the overarching enquiry question later on. You can see an example of these 'Record' instructions here. They will always be in blue text with blue lines above and below them.

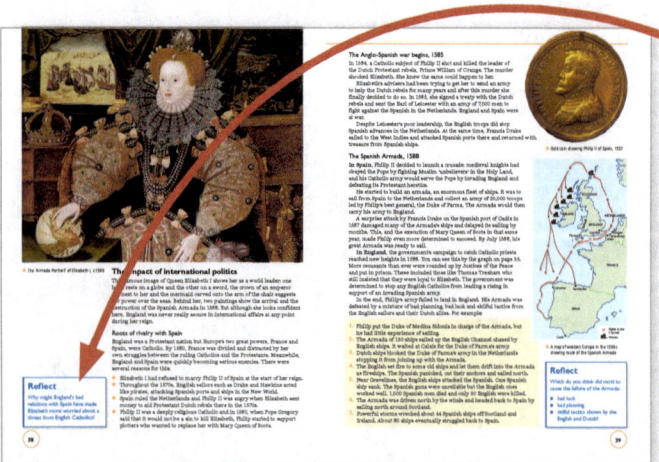

Reflect tasks

At regular intervals we will set a 'Reflect' task to prompt you to think carefully about what you are reading. They will look like the example shown here.

These Reflect tasks help you to check that what you are reading is making sense and to see how it connects with what you have already learned. You do not need to write down the ideas that you think of when you 'reflect', but the ideas you get may help you when you reach the next Record instruction.

Introduction

Review tasks

Each enquiry ends by asking you to review what you have been learning and use it to answer the overarching question in some way. Sometimes you simply answer that one question. Sometimes you will need to do two or three tasks that each tackle some aspect of the main question. The important point is that you should be able to use the ideas and evidence you have been building up through the enquiry to support your answer.

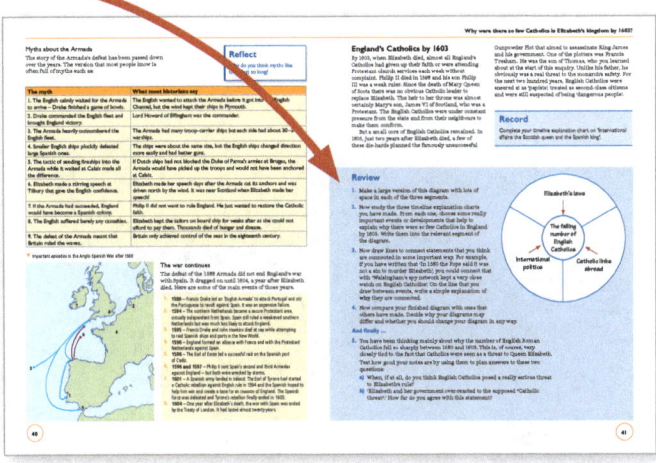

Closer looks

Between the enquiries you will find pages that provide a 'closer look' at some aspect of the theme or period you are studying. These will often give you a chance to find out more about the issue you have just been studying in the previous enquiry, although they may sometimes look ahead to the next enquiry.

We may not include any tasks within these 'closer looks' but, as you read them, keep thinking of what they add to your knowledge and understanding. We think they add some intriguing insights.

One very important final point

We have chosen enquiry questions that should help you get to the really important issues at the heart of each period you study, but you need to remember that the examiners will almost certainly ask you different questions when you take your GCSE. Don't simply rely on the notes you made to answer the enquiry question we gave you. We give you advice on how to tackle the examination and the different sorts of question you will face on pages 98 to 105.

England in 1580

▲ A reconstruction of the *Golden Hind* at sea, c.1987

This is a full-sized, modern replica of the *Golden Hind*, the ship in which the Elizabethan sailor, Francis Drake, famously sailed around the world. The original ship, like the replica, was just 31 metres long. It set off on its voyage from Plymouth in December 1577. When it returned on 26 September 1580, its holds were packed with Spanish treasure, stolen for the Queen.

It is hard to imagine but Drake and his crew of 80 men were completely out of touch with events in England for all that time. There was no ship radio or mobile telephone technology. As the ship drew close to English land for the first time in almost three years, Drake's mind must have been racing with questions, but one mattered more than all the others. He saw a fisherman mending his nets and leant out over the rails of the *Golden Hind*, calling out ...

'Is the Queen still alive?'

Drake could not take this for granted. Elizabeth had nearly died of smallpox in 1562 and plague could strike anyone at any time. (In fact it was raging in Plymouth even as he called out his question.) She was 47 years old by now and many women died by that age in the sixteenth century. But even if she were alive, maybe she had married. If so, who was her husband? A French duke? An English earl? Drake would need to win his favour or his career could be over.

The fisherman gave his reply: the Queen was alive and well – and unmarried.

Introduction

Drake would have been delighted. Elizabeth meant so much to her people. Each year, on 17 November, they celebrated the anniversary of the day when she became queen in 1558. She and her chosen advisers had guided the nation so carefully since then. In these Accession Day festivities, church bells rang, bonfires blazed, fireworks exploded. And there were church services and sermons too. Everyone was reminded that this was God's chosen queen!

But Drake may have wondered …

'Which queen is alive? Is it Queen Elizabeth Tudor or Queen Mary Stuart?'

If Elizabeth's heir, Mary Queen of Scots, had somehow become Queen of England, Drake's career would be over. He should simply turn his ship around and head back out to sea. As a firm Protestant, he could not serve a Roman Catholic like Mary and she would not want him to. If she were the Queen, the churches he could see in Plymouth and every church in the land would have gone back to the old Latin service of Mass. In Drake's eyes this would be a return to the superstitious beliefs of the Middle Ages. Worse still, Mary would have allowed the Pope to control the nation's religion. It was unthinkable.

All was well: it was Queen Elizabeth, not Queen Mary who ruled.

As Drake's ship approached the harbour and he saw more and more signs of life going on, another question must have formed in his mind:

'How much has life in England changed during my three years away?'

Drake might have looked closely at the roofs of Plymouth for signs of change. When he left in 1577 a new book had described a 'Great Rebuilding' of England. Old buildings were being knocked down and smart new ones, with modern brick chimneys, were taking their place. Only the rich could afford these of course. Poverty was becoming a serious problem when Drake left the country. Maybe Plymouth had built one of the new 'houses of correction' where the poor could be put to work rather than be left to beg or steal.

Most people on land looked busy enough: people were probably carrying on with their daily business much as always. Most would be working on the land to grow food while others were making, buying and selling goods in the towns. Maybe merchants were trading in new goods from foreign lands using routes opened up by English navigators, including many of Drake's own friends.

It was not all work of course. People would still be enjoying their usual pastimes: singing, dancing, drinking and watching bears or bulls defend themselves against dogs. And what about theatres? In the year before Drake left, two of these extraordinary new buildings had appeared in London. They were very popular with the rich and poor alike. But maybe nothing had come of this. Maybe they were just a passing fad.

And with thoughts of London, Drake must have prepared in his mind for the journey he would soon make, by horse, to visit the Queen at Whitehall or Richmond, or whichever great palace she and her splendid court were staying in. He would take packhorses loaded with just some of the treasure he had stolen from her Spanish enemies. Queen Elizabeth would be delighted. It was good to be back. 'Long live the Queen!'

▲ The port of Plymouth in Devon from a drawing made c.1540

1

Majesty

How did Elizabeth use her power?

▲ Elizabeth I in procession through the streets of London. Painted c.1601, probably by Robert Peake

There is no doubt who is the centre of attention in this remarkable picture. It is Her Majesty, Queen Elizabeth I of England. She looks remarkably upright and youthful at the age of 66. In her stunning white silk dress, woven with gold thread and covered in precious gems, she is lifted high above her loyal and loving subjects. As she makes her way through the streets of London, she is bathed in sunlight from the heavens above. It is a scene carefully designed to show her perfection, her popularity and her power.

Reflect

How has the artist tried to suggest Elizabeth's 'perfection, popularity and power'?

How did Elizabeth use her power?

The Enquiry

The painting on page 8 certainly creates a strong impression of Elizabeth I's majesty and power. But image and reality are not always the same. In this enquiry you will be discovering what powers over her people Queen Elizabeth really had, how she used them and why she used them in that way.

Historians cannot agree about this. They have reached many different interpretations over the years. Some have been quite critical of Elizabeth and the way she used her power. In his book *Elizabeth I*, historian Christopher Haigh called her both 'a bully' and 'a show-off'.

As you work through the enquiry you will be asked to identify evidence that will help you decide whether or not you agree with Haigh's view.

Make notes in a table like this:

| Was Elizabeth I a bully and a show-off? ||
| Reasons for agreeing | Reasons for disagreeing |

The enquiry is divided into these three parts:

- Elizabeth and her court
- Elizabeth and her parliament
- Elizabeth and her people.

Elizabeth and her court

Government through patronage

Today, elected politicians govern our nation. Every four or five years there is a general election when voters in each area decide who will represent them as members of parliament. The largest group in Parliament then forms a government until there is another election. This is a system of democracy, where power comes from the bottom up.

In the time of Elizabeth I, it was very different. Power came from the top down by a system known as 'patronage'. God appointed the monarch (the king or queen). The people were expected to be loyal to their God-given ruler and Elizabeth took every opportunity to remind her subjects of this fact in her speeches.

Just as God had chosen the Queen and had given her great power, so the Queen could choose whoever she wanted to help her rule the kingdom. She had far greater powers of patronage than any of her subjects. Elizabeth usually gave positions of power to wealthy nobles – and took these positions away if they upset her.

These nobles then gave responsibility and official jobs to the gentry. This group was mainly made up of knights, lawyers and rich merchants. The gentry took responsibility for watching over the population in their own locality and working to keep society running smoothly.

It's who you know

Patronage meant that friendship and favour mattered more than qualifications or talent. Personal relationships were at the heart of government, especially personal relationships with the Queen. This is why every noble wanted a place at Elizabeth's royal court and why Elizabeth made it very clear that she was the centre of attention.

Record

Start to make notes in your table. Use both columns if you can.

▼ The Elizabethan hierarchy and the system of patronage

GOD
grants power and status to…

the Queen
grants rewards and official jobs to…

the nobles and bishops
grant rewards and official jobs to…

the gentry
(knights, lawyers, merchants)
help the Queen and nobles to control…

everyone else

Rewards →
Loyalty ←

The court

The court was a gathering of nobles and higher gentry favoured by the Queen. It met wherever Elizabeth was staying, with her hundreds of servants and guards. Elizabeth's main London palace was at Whitehall but she had over 60 residences in total. The palaces she used most often were at Whitehall, Windsor, Richmond, Greenwich and Nonsuch. She rarely stayed more than a few weeks in any one place, partly because the drains could not cope with longer visits.

The Queen decided which nobles would have the honour of joining her at court. Her most favoured courtiers were given accommodation. Others were told to find lodgings nearby. Some even built their own grand London houses near Whitehall.

A Privy Chamber (Elizabeth's own rooms)
B Great Hall
C Council Chamber
D Banqueting House
E Tilt Yard (where jousts were held)

Reflect

Find ...
- the Queen's private stairs from the River Thames
- deer in St James's Park
- the Old Palace, where the Houses of Parliament now stand.

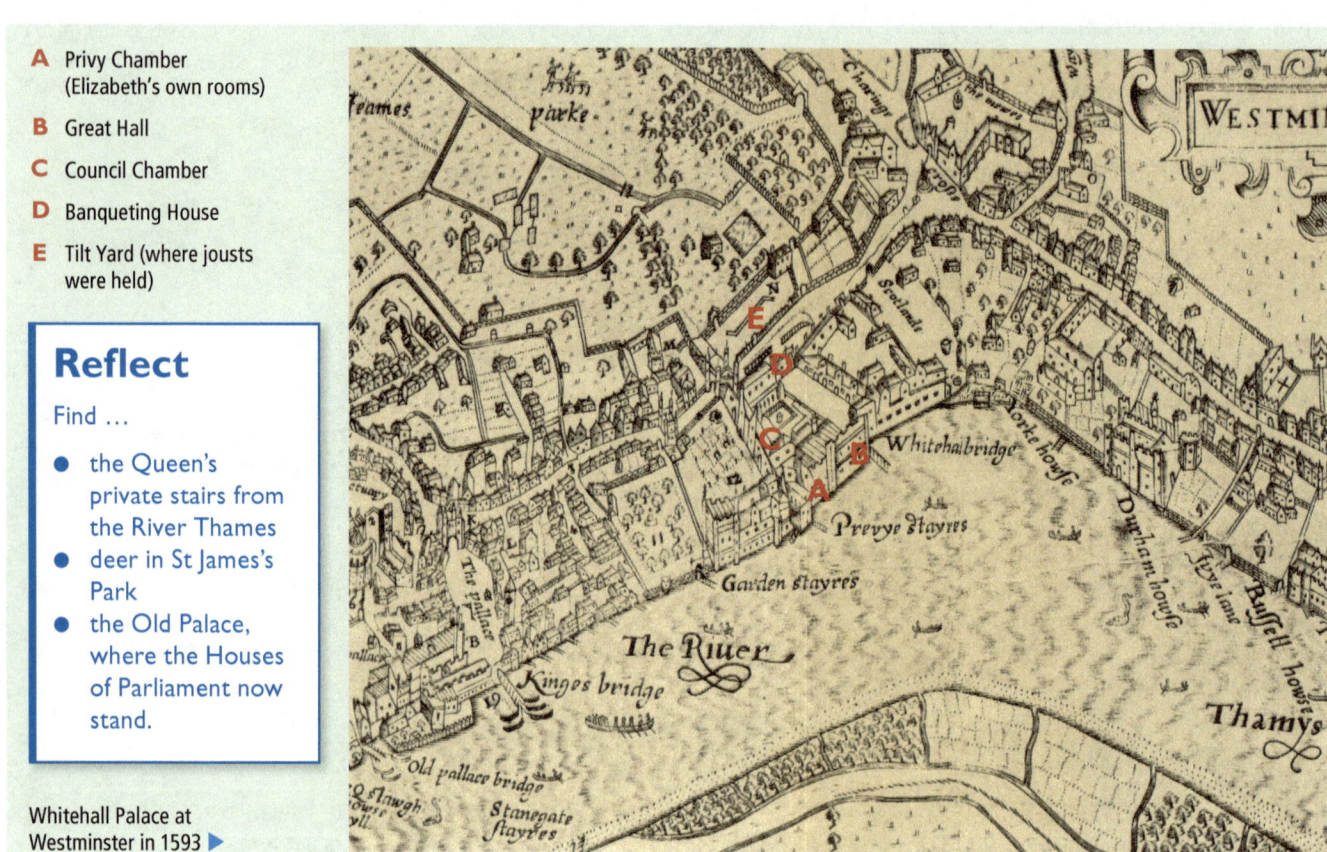

Whitehall Palace at Westminster in 1593 ▶

The courtiers

The painting on page 8 gives an idea of what these courtiers were like and how they built their power. Elizabeth liked to be seen in public. She knew that her predecessor Mary I had been criticised for isolating herself from her people. For many years people thought the picture showed the Queen going on procession to a grand house. But in fact the painting captures a very specific incident.

In 1866, an art historian discovered a letter written in 1600. It described how Elizabeth had just attended the wedding of two young courtiers at Blackfriars in London. He showed that the two figures in white behind the Queen are actually the bride and groom, Anne Russell and Henry Somerset. Each belonged to a noble family. The man standing in front of Elizabeth was the groom's father, the Earl of Worcester. In 1601, Elizabeth granted him an important job at court. He had this painting made to flatter the Queen, thank her for her patronage and to boast about his powerful court connections. Many of his closest court friends and relations are shown near the front of the picture.

Reflect

1. How does the painting on page 8 help us to understand patronage and the Tudor hierarchy?
2. Does the painting help us to decide whether Elizabeth was a bully and a show off?

How did Elizabeth use her power?

Business and pleasure

When the full court met it was quite a spectacle. Elizabeth's father Henry VIII had always used the court to show his power, but Elizabeth did the same with even more glamour. If the Queen was at Whitehall there would be:

- dances, plays, and musical performances in the Great Hall
- feasts in the Banqueting House
- open-air sermons in the main courtyard
- jousting tournaments in the tilt yard
- hunting expeditions in St James's Park.

Elizabeth was highly educated and was genuinely interested in art, religion, dance and sport. She loved to be seen dancing or to be heard speaking to ambassadors in their own language or Latin. She prided herself in her ability to ride and hunt. But court events mixed business with pleasure. Elizabeth used them to impress her nobles with her wealth, power and personality, while the nobles were looking to gain from her patronage.

Catching the Queen's eye

Nobles had great influence in their lands around the country. The Queen relied on them to keep the peace and to let her know the mood among her people. But they needed the Queen even more than she needed them. Although hundreds of nobles attended court, relatively few gained positions of real power. A well-worded remark in a rare conversation with Elizabeth, or an impressive display at a dance or in a tournament could open the way to a rewarding career. If a nobleman was clearly in favour with the Queen he could more easily build a network of his own loyal supporters among the gentry to keep his lands and wealth secure. If he lost the Queen's favour these people might seek patronage from other leading families. With growing interest in women's history, historians are now beginning to explore how nobles' wives helped to build and maintain these networks.

Balancing act

Elizabeth could have restricted her use of patronage to just a few noble families, but she preferred to offer titles, jobs, grants and pensions more widely. She tried to keep the support of all of them, as it was dangerous to allow separate groups of nobles to join forces against each other. Earlier Tudor monarchs had serious problems when rival groups, or factions as they were called, plotted to increase their power. Elizabeth used favour and firmness to balance different groups at court. Although she was a Protestant, for example, she allowed some Catholic noble families to attend court so that she did not lose their loyalty entirely. Patronage had to be handled with care and self-discipline.

> **Reflect**
>
> Why do you think Elizabeth held so many different types of event at court?

▼ Queen Elizabeth and courtiers on a hunt. From a popular manual on hunting, first published in 1575. The man kneeling before the Queen is the book's author. He has shown himself seeking patronage.

> **Record**
>
> Use pages 10 to 11 to add more notes to your table.

Record

As you read this page, add more ideas to your table.

The Privy Chamber

Elizabeth's household was at the heart of the court. Wherever she went she would spend most of the day in her Privy (private) Chamber talking, reading, playing music, playing card games or enjoying the company of her pet dogs, birds and apes.

A small group of ladies-in-waiting looked after the Queen. One was Anne Russell, the young bride from the painting on page 8. The women usually came from favoured noble families. They had to show complete loyalty to the Queen. Elizabeth once broke the finger of a lady-in-waiting who married without her permission. Elizabeth ordered the ladies-in-waiting to keep her informed about court conversations and opinions. Some earned money from nobles for praising their qualities to Elizabeth.

Elizabeth would sometimes conduct royal business from her Private Chamber. Only her most trusted courtiers were invited to discuss business with her in her own rooms. Some of the men shown standing behind Elizabeth belong to the small group of advisers that did more than anyone else to help the Queen govern her country: the Privy Council.

▼ Elizabeth I meets ambassadors from the Netherlands, c.1570

The Privy Council

This group of the Queen's most trusted courtiers met almost every day, although it was rare for them all to attend. Its main job was to offer her advice on matters including finance, trade, law enforcement and defence. Even if Elizabeth decided to reject their advice, they still faithfully put her chosen policies into action.

Privy councillors were selected directly by the Queen and could be dismissed by her at any time. Earlier Tudor monarchs had allowed individual councillors to gain too much power or had allowed the council to ignore their wishes. Elizabeth tried to avoid similar problems by:

- limiting the council to about nineteen members, with just seven or eight at most meetings
- appointing councillors with different viewpoints, leaving herself free to decide between them
- sometimes attending small meetings herself
- showing her fierce temper for no apparent reason
- dismissing councillors from court if they offended her
- discussing policies with courtiers who were not councillors
- encouraging loyalty by flattering privy councillors and rewarding them with jobs that allowed them to grow rich
- refusing to marry her beloved Robert Dudley, the Earl of Leicester, a leading member of the Privy Council.

Reflect

What is the difference between the Privy Chamber and the Privy Council?

▲ A painting of a meeting of the Privy Council in 1604, just after Elizabeth had died. This group of councillors was chosen by her successor, King James I. His Secretary of State, Robert Cecil, is at the bottom right corner.

How did Elizabeth use her power?

Elizabeth's secretaries of state

The official who organised the work of the Privy Council was the Secretary of State. We can learn a lot about how Elizabeth used her power by looking at the careers of two men who served in this role. They both came from gentry families. Elizabeth believed that highly educated gentry were better at day-to-day government than nobles.

> **Record**
> Use what you learn about Walsingham and Cecil to add more notes to your table.

◀ Sir Francis Walsingham painted c.1589.

◀ Sir William Cecil, Lord Burghley painted c.1587. You can see his son Robert, who took over as Secretary of State in 1598, in the painting on page 12.

Sir Francis Walsingham
(Secretary of State, 1572–90)

Background: Well-educated lawyer. Spoke several languages.

Religion: A strong Puritan. Believed English Catholics were a threat to the nation's stability and must be speedily repressed. Wanted to support Protestant rebels in Scotland and the Netherlands so that they would be allies against Catholic Spain.

Character: Cold and distant. Never tried to flatter or charm the Queen. Nicknamed 'The Moor', as he had dark hair and displayed the sort of secrecy and cunning that Tudors associated with the growing power of the Muslim Ottoman Empire.

His view of his role: Firmly believed he was a servant of the state, not the personal servant of the Queen. Sometimes used Parliament or courtiers to pressurise the Queen, such as when he persuaded her to drop her plan to marry the Duke of Anjou in 1580.

How Elizabeth responded to him: Admired his appetite for work. Valued his complete loyalty. Respected his direct, honest advice.

But … Was enraged when he spoke too directly: once threw a slipper at his head for daring to criticise her. Was angered by his impatience in the early 1580s when she felt he was rushing her into repressing English Catholics and sending troops to aid Protestants in the Netherlands. Never warmed to him as a person but often ended up doing what he advised in the interests of her people.

Death: Had a fit, probably caused by exhaustion. The Queen still sent him work and four days later, on 7 April 1590, he died. Elizabeth showed no obvious sign of grief and turned to her former Secretary of State, William Cecil to take on the role again.

Sir William Cecil, Lord Burghley
(Secretary of State, 1558–72 and 1590–98)

Background: A gentry family. Well-educated lawyer.

Religion: A moderate Protestant but favoured Puritans more than Elizabeth did. Also more ready to repress English Catholics than she was. Tried hard to avoid involvement in foreign religious disputes as that could lead to expensive wars.

Character: An intelligent, serious, thoughtful man but capable of charming courtiers and ambassadors as well as the Queen. Elizabeth called him her 'spirit', a nickname that suggests she and he were in tune on most matters.

His view of his role: Very similar to Walsingham, Cecil was never a mere 'yes-man' to the Queen. Used Parliament and courtiers to try to change the Queen's mind on some issues such as the need to execute Mary Queen of Scots in 1587.

How Elizabeth responded to him: Delighted by his classical education. Trusted him more than any other adviser. Shared his cautious approach to decision-making and desire to avoid expensive wars. Expected him to work extremely long hours, which he did. Continued to consult him when he was Lord Treasurer, 1573–90.

But … Once rebuked him by telling him that she had 'lifted him from the dirt and was able to cast him down again'. Refused to see him for months in 1587 when she believed he had effectively tricked her into executing Mary Queen of Scots.

Death: Died of exhaustion in 1598, aged 77. Elizabeth wept bitterly at the news. She turned to William's son Robert to take over as her new Secretary of State.

The rebellion of the Earl of Essex

In the 1590s, Elizabeth's normal careful control over faction broke down. The crisis followed the arrival of a newcomer at court.

The Queen's new favourite

Robert Devereux, the Earl of Essex, first appeared at Elizabeth's court in 1584 when he was about eighteen years old. Elizabeth was 51. His youthful strength, good-looks and skills at jousting and hunting added glamour to the court, and he soon became the Queen's new favourite. In 1587, Elizabeth spent a lot of time with him in the royal household, organising hunts and royal visits. They would spend hours together talking and playing cards until the early hours of the morning.

> **Reflect**
>
> Do you think Elizabeth was showing off by favouring the Earl of Essex?

Essex was an ambitious soldier. In 1589, he angered Elizabeth by defying her wishes and joining Sir Francis Drake's attack on the Portuguese city of Lisbon. He upset her again in 1590 when he married without asking her permission. This broke the custom of the court, but the Queen forgave him for both offences. In 1593, his military skill and knowledge of foreign affairs won him a place on the Privy Council.

Rivalry in the Privy Council

By the 1590s, Elizabeth was growing old. She had no husband and no named heir. The country was weakened by war with Spain, rebellion in Ireland, high taxes and bad harvests. Just when England needed strong leadership, a power struggle developed at court.

William Cecil expected his son, Robert, to follow him as the Queen's most trusted adviser. But this was the position that Essex wanted.

At first Essex and the Cecils managed to work together but that changed in 1596 after Essex led a successful attack on the Spanish port of Cadiz. He returned to huge public acclaim. Maybe this popularity made Elizabeth jealous. Maybe she preferred Robert Cecil's suggestion of a money-saving peace with Spain. Whatever the reasons, she made Robert Cecil her new Secretary of State. Essex was outraged and built an opposition faction at court. In June 1598, in a meeting where Elizabeth was clearly favouring Cecil, Essex rudely turned his back on her. She punched him on the ear and he started to draw his sword, but stopped himself just in time and stormed out of the room. For this he was banned from court for two months, returning soon after William Cecil died. Elizabeth knew that she needed Essex's skills as a soldier. She also missed him.

Failure in Ireland and crisis at court

In an effort to impress the Queen, Essex led an expedition to put down a rebellion in Ireland. He left in March 1599. He failed to crush the rebellion but still dared to award knighthoods to some of his followers in the name of the Queen. Elizabeth sent him a fierce rebuke. Essex then abandoned his army in Ireland and sailed back to London.

On 28 September 1600, when his ship arrived, he rushed directly to the court and forced his way into Elizabeth's bedchamber. At first she appeared to accept this astonishing behaviour but then banned him from court within just a few hours. She took away all his government jobs. This left him bankrupt.

The rebellion of 1601

For years, Essex had been working to win the favour of James VI of Scotland, who was next in line to the English throne. He hoped to be the new king's leading minister after Elizabeth's death. Now he tried to make the Queen restore his own wealth and power at court or give up her throne to James.

In January 1601, Essex started to gather large groups of supporters at his London home. The dangerous mix included courtiers who were out of favour and unemployed soldiers. In February, he arranged for a production of Shakespeare's play *Richard II* at the Globe Theatre in London. This included a scene where the king was forced to give up his throne. Essex seemed to be threatening Elizabeth.

The Queen sent four privy councillors to arrest Essex, but he locked them in his house and took to the streets of London. He rode through the city to Whitehall with 300 supporters and clearly expected the mass of the people to join him. They did not. The rebellion collapsed and he was arrested.

The Queen now made an example of him for all to see: on 25 February 1601, Essex was beheaded at the Tower of London, guilty of treason against his queen and country.

▶ A sixteenth century executioner's axe

How did Elizabeth use her power?

▲ The Earl of Essex in his finest tournament outfit, c.1595

Reflect
Films, novels, television dramas and even operas have been made about Elizabeth and Essex. Why do you think it has been such a popular theme?

Record
Finish this section on 'Elizabeth and her court' by adding more notes to your table. Use evidence from page 14 to give reasons for agreeing or disagreeing that Elizabeth was a bully and a show-off.

Record

Use pages 16 to 18 to consider whether Elizabeth bullied or showed off to Parliament. Add your ideas to your table.

Elizabeth and her parliaments

Parliament had far less power in Tudor times than it does today. The Privy Council met almost every day, but Parliament only met when the monarch called its members together. Elizabeth used Parliament less than earlier Tudors. In her reign of almost 45 years, Parliament only spent 35 months in debate and discussion.

When Parliament did meet it was composed of three elements:

1. The monarch, who only appeared at meetings on rare and special occasions.
2. The House of Lords, made up of the nobles and bishops.
3. The House of Commons, made up of members of the gentry who had been selected to attend by other wealthy citizens.

For most business, the Queen ruled by proclamations – royal orders that had the force of law. But if she wanted to make major changes to the laws of the land, introduce new punishments or to raise new taxes, Parliament had to meet to give her people's approval.

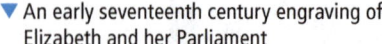

▼ An early seventeenth century engraving of Elizabeth and her Parliament

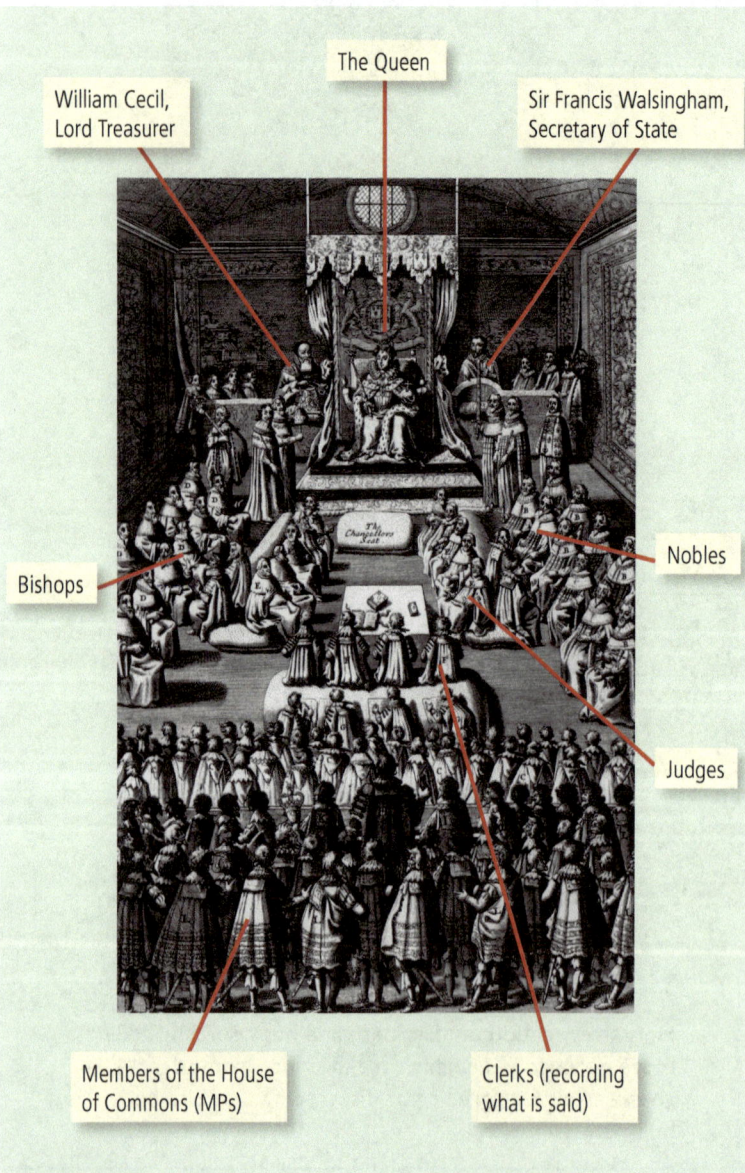

Controlling Parliament

When Parliament was sitting, Elizabeth set strict limits on what it could discuss. She insisted that it must not attempt to bring forward its own views on anything to do with religion, her marriage, the succession (who would take the throne when she died) and foreign policy. She said that these were matters for her alone to decide, just like any other monarch.

Elizabeth had various ways of trying to keep some control over what happened in Parliament:

- MPs were not really elected; they were selected. Local lords were expected to ensure that suitable people were chosen.
- Several privy councillors served as MPs in the House of Commons. Others sat in the House of Lords.
- The Privy Council organised daily business in Parliament.

Reflect

Which of these methods do you think would be most likely to help Elizabeth control Parliament?

If MPs did not do as she wished, the Queen could always reject a law by refusing to sign it or simply closing the Parliament. But her usual solution was to offer a compromise so that they won some of what they wanted but she still gained the taxes and laws that she needed.

Puritan opposition

Despite her attempts to control Parliament, Elizabeth found it increasingly difficult to stop MPs from discussing sensitive matters. Although patronage generally brought dependable gentry to Parliament, lords who were out of favour could select MPs who would speak against the Queen's policies. Even those privy councillors such as William Cecil and Walsingham used their influence over MPs to stir up debates that would make the Queen take their views on foreign policy or the succession more seriously. Although the great majority of MPs could be relied on to vote as the Queen wished, it was the ones who had grievances who tended to speak more often in debates.

Criticism in speech

Many of Elizabeth's noisiest and most troublesome critics in Parliament were Puritans. These were convinced Protestants who were delighted that England had broken away from the Roman Catholic Church, but who wanted more.

- They wanted Elizabeth to marry a Protestant prince and to make arrangements for her successor to be a Protestant as well.
- They wanted Elizabeth to change the way the Church was organised, doing away with bishops and allowing local church groups to choose their own leaders. This 'bottom-up' way of organising the Church was called Presbyterianism.
- They insisted that MPs had complete freedom of speech and that they must be allowed to say whatever they liked in Parliament without any fear of arrest or punishment.

Criticism in writing

Even when Parliament was not sitting, Puritans found other ways of voicing their concerns. In November 1579, a Puritan, John Stubbs, wrote a pamphlet criticising Elizabeth for considering a marriage with a French Catholic, the Duke of Anjou. The pamphlets were destroyed and Stubbs was arrested. At first Elizabeth wanted him hanged, but she then ordered a different punishment for Stubbs and for his colleague, William Page. An Elizabethan historian, William Camden, was an eye-witness:

> Upon a stage set up in the market place at Westminster, Stubbs and Page had their right hands cut off by the blow of a butcher's knife, with a mallet struck through their wrists. I can remember that Stubbs, as soon as his right hand was off, put off his hat with the left, and cried aloud, 'God save the Queen!'

▼ An illustration of Stubbs' punishment from a *History of Britain*, 1923

Reflect

Study the image above. How closely has the artist kept to the eye-witness account given by Camden? Does it matter if the artist's version is different?

After this brutal punishment, Stubbs was imprisoned. On his release in 1581, he carried on writing (presumably left-handed) and in 1589 he became an MP, continuing his criticism of the Queen in the House of Commons. But at no point did his criticism become treasonous. Unlike some Catholics, Puritans never openly expressed a desire to replace Elizabeth with another monarch.

The business of Parliament

The years between 1580 and 1603 were dominated by concerns over religion and war with Spain. This meant that Elizabeth needed to call Parliament more often. In the early seventeenth century, the very first historians of Elizabeth's reign praised the way she worked with Parliament. This was mainly because they thought that the kings of their own day, James I and Charles I, should learn from her example. In fact Elizabeth faced quite a lot of opposition in Parliament. This should not hide the fact that most of its day-to-day business in Parliament passed without any difficulty.

Opposition over religion

The Puritan MPs were a particular nuisance. In 1584 and again in 1586, the MPs demanded that the Church of England do away with bishops. (See page 17.) At first the other MPs ignored these demands but when they later decided to discuss the matter, Elizabeth banned the debate. Three MPs discussed the ideas outside Parliament and she had them imprisoned for a month. Two Suffolk Puritans had been hanged in 1583 for spreading similar views without the protection of being an MP.

In 1593, the Puritan MP Peter Wentworth urged Elizabeth to reassure her people and name a Protestant as her successor. Elizabeth was furious at his intrusion and imprisoned him in the Tower of London. He died there four years later.

Opposition over money

Many MPs were angry at how Elizabeth granted 'monopolies' to keep her courtiers happy. These monopolies allowed the courtier to be the only person to sell or make a product. Without any competition, the price usually went up.

In 1601, Elizabeth accepted that she had to cancel some monopolies. She made a famous 'Golden Speech' to Parliament that flattered MPs and boasted about how much she loved her people. This speech was printed by the Privy Council and issued for anyone to read. Its message was clear even though its language was dull. Most historians quote from a livelier account written soon afterwards by an MP who heard the speech.

> **An extract from an MP's account of Elizabeth's 'Golden Speech' to Parliament, 1601**
>
> I do assure you there is no prince that loves his subjects better ... No Queen will ever sit in my seat with more zeal to my country, or care for my subjects or who will sooner with willingness venture her life for your good and safety than myself. For it is my desire neither to live nor reign longer than my life and reign shall be for your good. And though you have had, and may have, many princes more mighty and wise sitting in this seat, yet you never had nor shall have, any that will be more careful and loving.

Reflect

1. Why do you think the speech has won the nickname 'Golden'?
2. Why do you think historians rarely quote from the official version of Elizabeth's 'Golden Speech'?
3. How does the nineteenth-century engraving make Elizabeth seem firmly in charge of her Parliament?

Record

Finish adding notes on whether Elizabeth was a bully or a show off in her treatment of Parliament.

▲ A nineteenth-century engraving of Elizabeth addressing her Parliament

Elizabeth and her people

Local government

Elizabeth was at the centre of government but she needed others to control the different areas of her kingdom where her three million subjects lived. The two most important roles were:

1. Lords Lieutenant

These were the officers who had overall responsibility for each county. The Earl of Worcester, shown with the Queen in the painting on page 8, was the Lord Lieutenant for Glamorgan and Monmouthshire. Elizabeth usually chose the most powerful nobleman in each area for this role. It was a great honour. He, or his deputy if he spent a lot of time at court, was expected to inform the Privy Council of any local problems. He also had to ensure that his county could provide well-trained, part-time soldiers to serve the Queen in an emergency. Within the counties, town affairs were run by councils elected by wealthy citizens.

2. Justices of the Peace

The men who did most to keep Elizabethan society running smoothly were the Justices of the Peace (JPs). There were about 40 in each county and it was up to them to keep Elizabethan society running smoothly. They usually came from educated gentry families. The Queen appointed them on the advice of a trusted courtier who knew them in person. Becoming a JP gave a man considerable influence in his locality, but the work was unpaid so he needed to have income from land or other business.

William Lambarde was a JP in Kent and wrote a 600-page book that described the many duties of a JP. They enforced the Poor Laws, collected taxes, set wage levels and arranged road repairs. They constantly received new orders from the Privy Council. Every three months at the quarter sessions, they judged crimes such as assault, burglary, alehouse brawls and slander against the Queen. Twice a year judges from London visited each county to hear more serious cases.

There was no police force to help the JPs keep law and order, and catching criminals was not easy. This is why national and local government largely relied on public punishments, such as the pillory, to deter people from wrongdoing. Minor crimes might be punished by a time in the public pillory. For more serious offences, Elizabeth encouraged the use of fines as this also added to her royal finances.

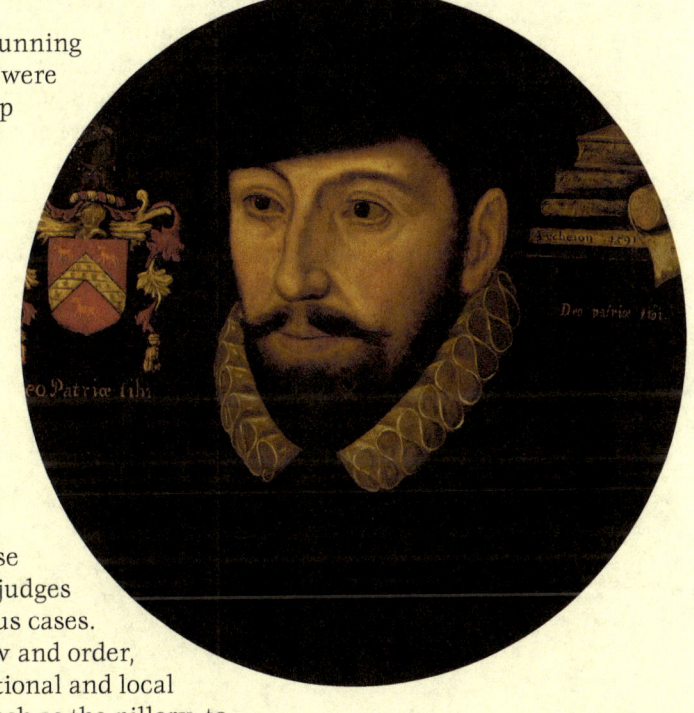
▲ William Lambarde JP, painted c. 1600

> **Record**
> Under the sub-heading 'Local government', add to your notes using ideas from this page.

Unjust justices and how Elizabeth responded

Some early histories of Elizabeth's reign relied too heavily on Lambarde's book as a source and created the impression that all JPs were loyal and hardworking. Many were, but recent research into local documents shows that other JPs were lazy and some favoured powerful families. For example, some turned a blind eye to Catholics who failed to attend church or deliberately under-estimated how much tax wealthy neighbours should pay. Elizabeth could remove a JP from office whenever she wished and she did so on many occasions. But she compromised if she thought the dismissal would make her dangerously unpopular in that JP's area.

Record

1. For each of the boxes on pages 20 to 22, make a summary card. On one side, do a simple drawing that sums up what the box is about. On the other side, say whether you think this shows Elizabeth using propaganda or censorship. Add examples to support your ideas.
2. When you have finished, add more notes to your table to help you decide whether Elizabeth was a bully and a show off.

Powers of persuasion

Elizabeth wanted her people to see her as a strong ruler who could keep the kingdom safe and wealthy. This involved two approaches:

1. Actively promoting a positive image of herself (propaganda).
2. Controlling the spread of other, conflicting views (censorship).

Even after considering all the evidence carefully, historians may disagree about which of these approaches Elizabeth used most. In this sense, interpretations of history are matters of opinion. The panels on pages 20 to 23 summarise how Elizabeth tried to persuade people that she was a fine queen.

Progresses and pageants

Each summer, when roads were in better condition and when outbreaks of plague might hit London, Elizabeth went with most of her advisers, officials and servants on a royal tour. They all stayed in the country houses of noblemen. These tours were known as progresses. As she travelled she made a point of being seen by as many of her people as possible. She tried to leave a lasting impression of majesty and affection. She sometimes stopped to speak with the people she passed.

Elizabeth expected her hosts to provide comfortable accommodation and impressive entertainment for her court. It was an expensive business. The engraving below shows a pageant held in her honour during her four-day stay with the Earl of Hertford in June 1591. The earl created an enormous artificial lake, castles and a warship. On the left of the picture, mermaids are playing music for the Queen on her throne. Hertford was flattering the Queen while showing his own education, wealth and power. Elizabeth saw advance plans for the plays and pageants and cut anything that might seem to criticise her.

▲ Elizabeth's kingdom

▲ Print showing entertainment on a royal progress, c.1591

Very few subjects ever attended these great entertainments so the Privy Council deliberately developed Accession Day pageants. On 17 November each year, towns and villages tried to outdo each other with bell-ringing and great bonfires, remembering the day when Elizabeth first took the throne.

Reflect

How does the map above show that Elizabeth needed more than royal progresses to show her wealth and power to her people?

How did Elizabeth use her power?

Publications and plays

There were never more than 60 printing presses in England in Elizabeth's reign. It was relatively easy for the Privy Council to censor publications they disapproved of, punishing the writers and printers severely. (See John Stubbs on page 17). They published their own books defending policies such as the execution of Catholic priests. Elizabeth's final speech to Parliament in 1601 (see page 18) was published by her own printer, Robert Barker, and was circulated within two days. The Privy Council was keen to spread the speech's message: she loved her people.

The Privy Council also encouraged others to spread favourable views of the Queen to all who could read. Elizabeth helped Edmund Spenser's epic poem *The Faerie Queene* to become popular as it praised a queen very like her.

Nobles knew that Elizabeth enjoyed plays and often brought acting groups to court. Their performances often showed how kings and queens gave society order and prosperity. If the Queen liked a play, it would soon appear in print. Educated people around the country bought copies and arranged performances in their own homes. The government encouraged this.

The Queen and her government allowed favourable plays to spread. The Spanish Ambassador was upset at the way his king, Philip II, and the Pope were mocked in English plays. The government allowed this but they briefly shut down London's theatres in 1597 when a play seemed to criticise the Queen. The theatres soon re-opened and the playwrights only spent a short time in prison.

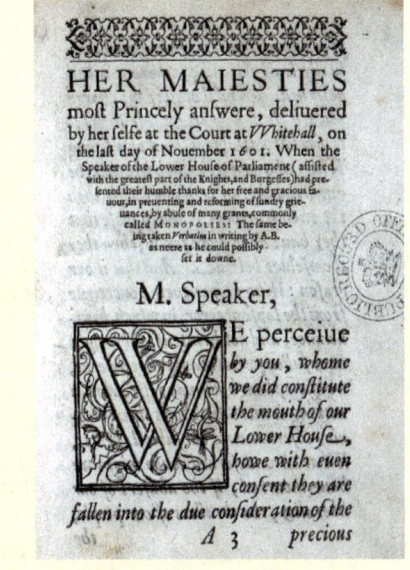

▲ A printed copy of the official version of Elizabeth's 'Golden Speech' to Parliament, 1601

Portraits and pennies

Very few of Elizabeth's people ever saw a painting of her. Most Elizabethans probably gained an impression of what their queen looked like from their coins: it was hardly a flattering picture.

About 135 paintings of Elizabeth survive from her time but there must have been many more. The Queen and her Privy Council did relatively little to spread her image, but they certainly tried to control the number and quality of the portraits that could be seen:

- In 1584, they considered controlling her image by giving just two artists, Nicholas Hilliard and George Gower, the sole right to make miniature and larger portraits of the Queen. The idea was dropped.
- In 1596, they ordered that portraits of the Queen that caused her 'great offence' should be burned. These included any where she looked old and likely to die without an obvious heir to her throne.
- Also in 1596, a new pattern of Elizabeth's face was created to replace one issued in 1575. The new pattern made Elizabeth look far younger than she was. This was to hide the fact that she was 63 years old with blackened teeth and false hair.

The portrait on the right was found in a Sussex cottage where an Elizabethan farmer lived. In 1889, some Victorian workers were repairing the cottage. They removed a blackened panel from above the fireplace. When cleaned, it turned out to be this oil painting of Elizabeth. If a Tudor farmer owned it in the 1580s, then the Queen's image did reach quite a long way down society, but some historians cannot believe the painting was in the farmhouse at that date.

◄ An Elizabethan three halfpenny coin

▼ A portrait of Elizabeth I, c.1585

Most high-quality images of Elizabeth were made by and for the wealthy in society. Elizabeth expected all courtiers to wear miniature portraits of her, at least while they were at court. She had some miniatures made for her favourites but she never commissioned her own full-size portraits. That was an expensive business that she left to the courtiers themselves.

Portraits commissioned by courtiers tried to flatter the Queen. They often included emblems and symbols as a sort of code that educated Elizabethans would understand but that modern historians still interpret in very different ways. Some say they stress her purity like the Virgin Mary. Others say they try to show her strength as a Protestant queen sent by God. The symbols include:

Symbols	What they stood for
Tudor roses; crown; orb; sceptre; sword	Elizabeth's rightful place as queen
White clothing; pearls; thornless roses	Purity and strength
Ermine (an animal that Tudors believed would die rather than dirty its pure white fur)	Self-sacrifice and commitment to her people
Pelican (a bird that Tudors believed would peck at its own flesh to feed its young)	
Globe; fans with exotic feathers	English power overseas
Sunshine; rainbows	Peace and stability
Goddesses and women from Bible stories	God-given strength to rule

▲ The Ditchley portrait of Elizabeth I, painted c. 1592

This portrait was made for the Queen by Sir Henry Lee. He had served her at court for many years and had introduced the great jousting competition that was held at Westminster each Accession Day. This was the most splendid of all the Queen's court celebrations. When he retired in 1590 he went back to Oxfordshire to live with his mistress. The Queen was angry with him and made her displeasure public. Lee won his way back to favour by hosting a royal progress at his home at Ditchley in Oxfordshire where he showed off this portrait that he had commissioned. It shows Elizabeth standing tall over the kingdom, with her feet in Oxfordshire. The main message is about the Queen's forgiving nature and how she turns storms to glorious sunshine.

How did Elizabeth use her power?

Prayers and preaching

The law required everyone to attend church each Sunday and to use the same prayer book. At every service the worshippers would say this 'Prayer for the Queen's Majesty' (right). It reinforced in people's minds their duty of loyalty and gratitude to Elizabeth, God's chosen ruler.

A service of thanksgiving was held in every church each year on Accession Day. The Queen's carefully chosen church leaders wrote special sermons, prayers and songs for priests to use at these services. They thanked God for providing a strong Protestant queen and for protecting her from Catholic threats. All preachers had to have a government licence.

▼ An Elizabethan sermon, from the opening page of a Bible published c.1560

A 'Prayer for the Queen's Majesty'

O Lord, our heavenly father, high and mighty king of kings, lord of lords, the only ruler of princes … most heartily we beseech thee to behold our most gracious sovereign Lady Queen Elizabeth … Fill her plentifully with heavenly gifts; grant her in health and wealth long to live; strengthen her that she may vanquish and overcome all her enemies. And finally, after this life may she attain everlasting joy and felicity through Jesus Christ our Lord. Amen.

Reflect

Based on pages 20 to 23, which do you think Elizabeth used more: propaganda or censorship?

Record

Finish adding notes on whether Elizabeth was bully or a show off in her use of local government and her 'powers of persuasion'.

Review

By now you should have lots of examples that you can use to help you decide whether you agree with Christopher Haigh that Elizabeth I was a 'bully' and a 'show-off'.

First read the views of another historian, Susan Doran, below. Then do the tasks that follow.

> At times Dr Haigh seems to be taken in by Elizabeth's love of theatricality. Always on public display, she deliberately played a part for public consumption and it is disputable whether or not her behaviour on any single occasion was spontaneous or contrived. Was she as evil-tempered, for example, as Dr Haigh declared, or were at least some of her public rages an instrument of public management?

a) How does Susan Doran disagree with Christopher Haigh?
b) What words does Susan Doran use to suggest that she does not disagree completely with Haigh?
c) Now write your own summary of what you have decided. Be sure to look at both sides of the question by giving reasons for agreeing that Elizabeth was a bully and a show-off, as well as reasons for disagreeing with that view. At the end, be sure to give your own conclusion and your main reasons for reaching this judgement.
d) Compare your summary with those of fellow students. How similar are your views? Why might they differ?

CLOSER LOOK 1

Elizabeth in film and on television

Historians are not the only ones who interpret the past. Playwrights, novelists and film or television directors have often set their stories in the past, blending historical fact with their own inventions or insights. They call this their 'artistic licence', their freedom to interpret the past and to achieve their aims without keeping to the strict methods used by historians.

These 'popular' television and film dramas or comedies can reach enormous audiences. They can spark an interest in the past and they can be very moving and entertaining. But they can also mislead. Someone once said that most people do not learn history, we just catch it in the same way that we might catch a cold: without any effort on our part we are exposed to a view of the past and it takes hold of our minds.

In dramas, we are not always aware of what is fact and what is fiction, or of what has been left out or what has been exaggerated, or why the director has done this. We may also be unaware of how events, ideas and values of the time when the programme or film was made have affected its message. Without realising it, we may get a distorted view of the past.

▲ Glenda Jackson as Elizabeth in her old age in *Elizabeth R*, 1971

Elizabeth on screen

Elizabeth Tudor was such an unusual woman, living through so many dramatic events that her life story has often been retold on screen. Here are summaries of three well-known examples.

Elizabeth R

In 1971, the BBC made six dramas that took viewers through the events of Elizabeth's life from her teenage years to her death. The same actress, Glenda Jackson, played Elizabeth from her youth to old age. The series received enormous praise for the way it tried to take historical scholarship seriously. Characters often spoke words taken more or less unchanged from documents made at the time. Its central theme was the way Elizabeth had to use her wits and her sense of duty as queen to operate in a man's world and to steer herself and her country through dangerous times. It was made at a time when the women's liberation movement was establishing itself and some say Elizabeth seems too much in control of the men around her. One historian, Susan Doran, wrote that the true Elizabeth 'was not the Glenda Jackson of *Elizabeth R* whose snarl could tame a cast of courtiers'.

Elizabeth in film and on television

Blackadder II and 'Queenie'

In 1986, Queen Elizabeth appeared as a central character in the comedy series *Blackadder II*. Historians made no fuss about its obvious inaccuracies. It was clearly not to be taken seriously as it was made purely to entertain and amuse.

The actor Miranda Richardson portrays Elizabeth as 'Queenie', a spoiled little girl, who must always get her own way. She has a terrible temper and has a crush on a new man in most episodes. In an interview on how she developed the character of 'Queenie', Richardson said:

I think I knew that this was someone with a lot of power but far too young to deal with it. I thought of her as someone who everyone was saying 'Yes' to ... always knowing they could have their head snipped off on a whim.

Clearly this was very different from the carefully researched *Elizabeth R*, but it is interesting to see how Miranda Richardson drew on the history she had 'caught' to develop the character of the Queen.

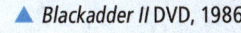
▲ *Blackadder II* DVD, 1986

Elizabeth

This film was made in 1998 by director Shekhar Kapur. He shows a young Elizabeth becoming caught up in the world of politics. She sees that she must choose between her personal desires and her duties as queen. The final scenes show her making a conscious decision to become a 'Virgin Queen' to her people, like the Virgin Mary is to Catholics. The picture below shows her appearing for the first time before her court in her pure white dress, with her powdered white face. She wears a wig because she has cut off her long hair, like a nun taking a vow of obedience to God. She walks the room from a bright heavenly light. She has taken on the role of a goddess, a divine ruler.

Kapur said his film was an exploration of power. He had researched paintings of Elizabeth and the works of historians who for many years had written about the 'cult of the Virgin Queen'. Unfortunately, most historians now reject the idea that Elizabeth herself deliberately created this image. Even if she did, the image developed over many years and was only obvious much later in her reign than the film suggests. Kapur would not be bothered by this. He said that the film tried to explore emotions rather than the details of history.

The film has been highly praised for its story-telling, acting, costumes and fine photography. But Kapur has drastically altered historical timings and events, even showing Francis Walsingham as a murderer. He would claim that none of this matters. What do you think?

▼ Cate Blanchett as *Elizabeth*, 1998

2 'Dangerous people'
Why were there so few Catholics in Elizabeth's kingdom by 1603?

▲ 'The Forty Martyrs of England and Wales' by Daphne Pollen, 1968

This picture shows a scene that is entirely imaginary but it is based on grim truth. Against the background of the English countryside stands a hangman's scaffold. At the very centre of the image, on a household cupboard covered by a white linen cloth, stands a crucifix, with the figure of Christ dying on the cross.

Although the artist has brought 40 real people together in this painting, they never all gathered like this. Some of them had died before others were even born. The diverse mix includes men and women, English and Welsh, educated and uneducated, wealthy and humble. But they do have one thing in common: they were all Catholic martyrs. They were brutally executed for refusing to give up their Roman Catholic faith and for their loyalty to the head of their Church, the Pope.

This explains many of the strange features that appear in the painting:

- the Tower of London which is where many of these martyrs were held and tortured
- the scaffold which shows the ropes by which they were lifted and hanged
- the bonfire which is where their internal organs were burned in front of the large crowds who watched them die.

Despite these references to cruelty, pain and death, the artist has shown the group gathered rather like ghosts around the simple altar, looking calm and untroubled.

Why were there so few Catholics in Elizabeth's kingdom by 1603?

The painting was specially made for an event in 1970, almost 300 years after the last of the people in the picture was executed. At a special ceremony in Rome, Pope Paul VI declared the 40 people shown in the image to be official saints of the Roman Catholic Church. The group had been carefully selected to represent a far larger number of Catholics who were put to death in England and Wales between 1535 and 1679. Seven different monarchs ruled the country over that period but nineteen of the 40 martyrs in the picture were executed in the reign of just one ruler: Queen Elizabeth I.

In total, Elizabeth ordered the execution of at least 200 Roman Catholics during her reign. But these deaths do not explain why there were so few Catholics in her kingdom by 1603. Just before Elizabeth became queen in 1558, the vast majority of the nation's 3 million people were Roman Catholic. By 1603, when Elizabeth died, there were only about 40,000. In this enquiry you will learn how and why Elizabeth and her government felt threatened by the Roman Catholic faith of so many of her people and how they worked to remove it from her kingdom. Together they watched over one of the deepest and long-lasting shifts in British history, the move from Catholicism to Protestantism.

> **Reflect**
>
> People have described the painting as:
> - strange
> - ghostly
> - dream-like
> - quietly sinister.
>
> Which of these descriptions do you think best fits the painting and why?

The Enquiry

An Act of Parliament passed in 1593 described Roman Catholics in England and Wales as 'dangerous people'. Most of them would have been puzzled and alarmed to be described in this way. They were simply trying to get on with their lives as their parents and grandparents had done for centuries. But the world was changing around them and forces they could not control turned their religious faith into a political threat to the authority, and even the life, of their Queen. They had to change their ways or suffer the consequences.

Your challenge at the end of this enquiry is to produce a mind map that summarises the years between 1580 and 1603, showing the links between:

- Elizabeth's laws on religion and how they were enforced
- the work of English Catholics who spent time in exile overseas
- the world of international politics, especially the part played by Mary Queen of Scots and the kings of Spain.

As you learn about each of these, you should make notes using a timeline explanation chart like the one shown below. Start a new chart for each section so that you can compare them, side by side, at the end.

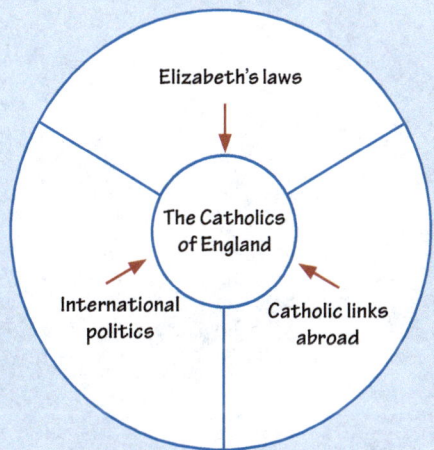

When your three timeline explanation charts are finished, you will review what they show and select from them the best evidence to explain why there were so few Catholics in England by 1603.

Then you will create your mind map, based on a large version of the diagram above. Your finished mind map will show the links between the three sections and how they combined to increase the supposed Catholic threat to the Queen and, as a result, to reduce so drastically the number of Catholics in England.

Section 1 – Elizabeth's laws and English Catholics		
Date	Event/development	How this affected English Catholics

Record

Start making the first of your timeline explanation charts (see page 26). As you read pages 28 to 30, look for key events and developments. For each one, note the date, describe briefly what happened and explain how you think it affected English Catholics.

Faith and enforcement: Elizabeth's laws and English Catholics, 1580–1603

This curious image shows Sir Thomas Tresham, a Catholic gentleman. In 1580, Thomas was 37 years old. He was a wealthy landowner and keen farmer in Northamptonshire. He came from a strong Catholic gentry family. Although they were all Catholics, Thomas and his family attended the parish church each Sunday and worshipped according the Protestant Book of Common Prayer. They were still Roman Catholics at heart but were prepared to go along quietly with the laws that had governed religion since the start of Elizabeth's reign in 1558. The two main laws were:

1. **The Act of Uniformity (1559)** – This said that all worship should be the same (uniform). Each week, everyone had to attend a church service that followed the Book of Common Prayer in English. Those who did not attend had to pay a fine.
2. **The Act of Supremacy (1559)** – This said that Elizabeth was the supreme governor of the Church in England. She was the head of the Church just as she was head of the state. Any Roman Catholic who insisted that the Pope was the head of God's Church on Earth was, in effect, a traitor for daring to challenge the Queen's supremacy over all her nation's affairs.

▲ Portrait of Thomas Tresham, 1585

Reflect

Which do you think mattered more to Elizabeth, the Act of Uniformity or the Act of Supremacy?

Unlike Thomas Tresham, many English Catholics had completely dropped their old faith by the 1570s. There were several reasons for this:

- Most priests accepted Elizabeth's changes.
- Weekly Protestant sermons gradually altered people's beliefs.
- Few Elizabethans could afford the fines for non-attendance at church.
- All marriages and baptisms had to follow the Protestant prayer book.

Millions of English Catholics, however, were still like Tresham. On the outside, they showed loyalty by attending Protestant church services. On the inside, they were still Catholics and loyal to the Pope, but they did nothing to challenge the Queen. Elizabeth was happy with this. She allowed Catholics to attend court and, in strong Catholic areas, she did not even insist that Justices of the Peace should strictly enforce church attendance. She believed that, given time, the English Catholic community would quietly die away.

Reflect

On the left of the image, a hand offers Tresham a globe, symbolising the world and its pleasures. What do the objects below the globe tell us about Tresham's 'wordly' interests?

Why were there so few Catholics in Elizabeth's kingdom by 1603?

Catholic resistance builds from 1580

Around 1580 the situation was changing. Elizabeth and her government could no longer sit quietly and wait for Catholicism to wither away. Thomas Tresham's story gives a sense of what was happening. For years he had been a 'church papist', attending church regularly as the law required. During the Protestant services, confident church papists made little attempt to hide their real feelings: some read old Latin prayer books to themselves, others used their rosary beads during the prayers and a few even refused to take Holy Communion. But Tresham had always made a good outward show of worshipping as the Queen wished. His loyalty brought rewards: even though his private Catholic faith was well known, Elizabeth had made him Sheriff of Northamptonshire in 1573.

Recusants

Then, sometime in 1580, Tresham became one of the Catholics who refused to attend church. These were known as 'recusants' from the Latin word for refuse. Recusants needed to be fairly wealthy as they had to pay a fine of 12d for each service they missed. This was about three or four days' wages for a labourer. Despite the fine, the numbers of recusants began to rise around 1580 as more Catholics stood up to be counted, disobeyed the rules about worship and posed a real threat to the Queen's authority.

Even after becoming a recusant, Tresham still proclaimed his complete loyalty to the Queen. But other Catholics went further and plotted to overthrow Elizabeth and to return her kingdom to Catholic ways. The four main responses of Catholics to Elizabeth's religious laws by 1580 are shown below:

> **Reflect**
>
> The right-hand side of the image of Thomas Tresham shows signs of his deepening Catholic faith.
>
> Look carefully, can you find:
>
> - signs of Christ's crucifixion
> - rosary beads
> - a chalice (cup) used in the service of Mass
> - a sign that Tresham was ready to die for his faith?

> **Reflect**
>
> Why might the presence of just a few plotters make life harder for all English Catholics?

Conformers

Number: A large proportion of English Catholics, especially in the south and east

Actions: Chose to drop their Catholic faith and to conform, that is to become Protestants

Reasons:
- It made life easier.
- They avoided the social and financial costs of hanging on to Catholicism.
- Persuasive sermons from Protestant preachers, with no Catholic priests to argue back, made people believe that the old Catholic ways were superstitious and corrupt.

Church papists

Number: Most English Catholics, especially in the north and west

Actions: Attended Protestant church services, but kept Catholic beliefs with some loyalty to the Pope

Reasons:
- They valued the centuries-old catholic teachings.
- It avoided social and financial costs of being a recusant.
- They hoped that the country would return to Catholicism when Elizabeth died as her successor would be the Catholic, Mary Queen of Scots.

Plotters

Number: Very, very few English Catholics, probably never more than two hundred or so

Actions: Usually refused to attend Protestant church services

Fiercely loyal to Catholic beliefs and to the Pope

Reasons:
- They valued the centuries-old catholic teachings.
- They believed Elizabeth was not the rightful queen ever since her excommunication in 1570.
- Were not prepared simply to wait for Elizabeth to die. They felt a duty to God and to the Pope to replace her with the Catholic, Mary Queen of Scots.

Recusants

Number: Several thousand English Catholics, especially in the north and west; usually wealthy

Actions: Refused to attend Protestant church services

Kept Catholic beliefs with some loyalty to the Pope

Arranged their own services of Mass

Reasons:
- They valued the centuries-old catholic teachings.
- Could afford to pay recusancy fines and had high social status especially with other Catholics.
- They hoped that the country would return to Catholicism when Elizabeth died as her successor would be the Catholic, Mary Queen of Scots.

> **Reflect**
>
> How would each of these measures have encouraged Catholics to give up their faith?

Tighter controls, 1581–85

Elizabeth's government had to find some way of ending the revival of Catholic recusancy. In **1581**, Parliament passed the **Act of Persuasions**. This:

- raised the fine for recusancy by 10,000 per cent to £20 per month, roughly the income of most landowning gentry families
- added an extra fine of £200 each year for persistent recusants
- imposed a fine of £66 on anyone who attended a service of Mass
- allowed the imprisonment of recusants who failed to pay their fines within three months
- said that anyone who persuaded a Protestant to become a Catholic was guilty of treason and should be put to death.

Only the wealthiest Catholics could pay these new fines. Thomas Tresham was one of these and so he still refused to attend church. This cost him both money and reputation. William Cecil ended his patronage of Tresham and added his name to a list of Catholics who were suspected of disloyalty to the Queen.

Arrests and imprisonment

In 1581, Tresham was arrested along with other influential Catholics. He was sent to prison in London. He was charged with allowing Catholic priests to stay secretly in his home. He explained that this might have happened without his knowledge as many people stayed at his house. He still swore that he was loyal to Queen Elizabeth, however, and was released after paying yet another fine.

Over the next fifteen years, Tresham, like many recusants from the gentry, was constantly in and out of prison. Each time they were released, these Catholics paid another fine but the richest still refused to attend church. Some even attended secret services of Mass in prison, taken by priests who were fellow prisoners. In 1582, four priests even broke into York prison to say Mass with the Catholics there. One was captured as they climbed out.

The government saw priests as the heart of the Catholic resistance. In **1585**, an **Act against Priests** allowed the death penalty for anyone who offered shelter or aid to a Roman Catholic priest. It also made it treasonable to be a priest. Acting on information from neighbours or informers, soldiers might appear at a Catholic house at any time and carry out a search. In 1585, Thomas Tresham organised a petition to the Queen promising the loyalty of her Catholic subjects. It made no difference. The arrests continued.

▼ This image shows English Catholics being arrested and taken to prison. It is from a book of Catholic propaganda that was published in Europe in 1592. In the upstairs room of a private home, soldiers arrest a priest who is saying Mass. The men of the house are being shoved through a doorway on the right, while the women and another priest are also being led away.

> **Reflect**
>
> How useful would this image be to a historian studying life for Catholics in Elizabethan England?

Why were there so few Catholics in Elizabeth's kingdom by 1603?

Greater suffering, 1586–1603

Financial suffering

The repression of Catholics tightened still further. The Queen wanted to increase her income from fining Catholics. In **1587**, another **Recusancy Act** allowed the government to take two-thirds of the land owned by any recusant who had fallen behind with paying fines. Even the wealthiest Catholics like Tresham were being driven into debt. Poorer Catholics suffered even more.

Physical suffering

In 1586, Margaret Clitherow, a butcher's wife from York, was accused of sheltering priests. She tried to avoid execution by refusing to plead either guilty or not guilty at her trial. But the law allowed her captors to encourage her to enter a plea. They did this by 'pressing': she was stretched out with a large, sharp stone beneath her back. A door, possibly from her own house, was placed over her and enormous weights were added. She still refused to plead and died as her ribcage burst and the air was pressed from her body.

In 1588, the Catholic king of Spain, Philip II, sent his Armada to invade England and return it to the Catholic faith. Elizabeth's government arrested all the most influential Catholics to stop them leading an uprising in England in support of the Spanish. Eleven Catholic laymen (that is not priests) were executed in 1588 for aiding priests or for encouraging Protestants to convert to Catholicism.

▲ This image shows how Margaret Clitherow became the first woman Catholic Martyr of Elizabeth's reign. It comes from a book of Catholic propaganda that was published in Europe in 1587.

Social suffering

Thomas Tresham was among those arrested in 1588. He was held at Ely in Cambridgeshire on and off over the next two years. On his release in 1590, he caught the mood of all Catholics when he described himself as 'disgraced, debased and scorned'. In **1593** the government added to Catholics' social isolation by passing the **Act Restraining Recusants**. This required Catholics over the age of sixteen to stay within five miles of their home at all times. It also banned them from holding large gatherings.

Elizabeth could rightly claim that she never made it illegal to hold Catholic beliefs, but by enforcing worship at Protestant church services, crippling them with debt and isolating them socially, her government was crushing the Catholic community just as Margaret Clitherow had been crushed in her prison cell.

Once again, Thomas Tresham serves as an illustration of what was happening to English Catholicism at this time. In 1599, he was in prison again but this time he was being held for debt, not for recusancy. He managed to outlive the Queen but when he died in 1605, his fortune was gone and so was the respect of his family name. He was still a Catholic, but that put him among a tiny minority, barely one or two per cent of the entire population. Despite the hardships he suffered for his faith, he declared his complete loyalty to Elizabeth and to her successor King James.

Reflect

Why might Elizabeth's government have wanted to restrict the freedom of Catholics to move around and meet each other?

Record

Complete your timeline explanation chart on 'Elizabeth's laws and English Catholics'.

Record

On a new sheet of paper, start making your second explanation chart as described on page 27. Use the section heading 'The work of English priests, 1580–1603'.

Reflect

Do you think it is possible for someone who is a 'saint' (living a good and holy life) to be a 'traitor', betraying his or her country?

Saints and traitors: the work of English priests, 1580–1603

The Pope and his priests

Most English priests who refused to accept Elizabeth's new Protestant Church in 1559 left the country and became exiles working in universities abroad.

Elizabeth must have been especially pleased that these exiles had left when, in 1570, Pope Pius V excommunicated (expelled) her from the Roman Catholic Church. He told English Catholics that she was therefore not the rightful queen of England and ordered them not to obey her laws. Without the leadership of their priests, very few English Catholics paid much attention to this.

The most important English priest in exile was William Allen. He saw how English Catholics desperately needed priests if they were to keep their faith and to worship God at the service of Mass. In the mid-1570s, largely thanks to his efforts, deeply committed young English priests started to arrive in England from France. This really worried Elizabeth's government.

There were two types of priest:

1. Seminary priests

These were young English Catholics who trained at seminaries (colleges) abroad. William Allen ran two seminaries by 1580. One was at Rheims in France and the other was at Rome in Italy. By 1603, 438 priests had been sent to England.

Seminary priests were trained to support Catholics in England, especially by leading them in services of Mass and hearing confessions of their sins. They were told not to try to convert Protestants to Catholic ways.

▲ Seminary priests praying with the Pope. From a Catholic book published in 1584

2. Jesuit priests

Jesuits were priests who were specially trained to persuade people either to become Catholics or to deepen their existing Catholic faith. Jesuits also had a direct loyalty to the Pope.

The first two Jesuits to return to England were Robert Persons (sometimes called Parsons) and Edmund Campion. They arrived in 1580 and they came in heavy disguise. This was a secret mission.

▲ Robert Persons and Edmund Campion from a Protestant propaganda book, 1627

Why were there so few Catholics in Elizabeth's kingdom by 1603?

The secret priests arrive in 1580

The Jesuits Robert Persons and Edmund Campion were smuggled in disguise into England in June 1580. They knew their lives were in danger. Two seminary priests had already been executed as traitors in 1577. In the eyes of the English government, all Catholic priests were traitors serving the Pope and challenging the rule of Elizabeth I.

Priests generally stayed at the country houses of wealthy gentry families, such as the Treshams, celebrating Mass and teaching Catholics. In 1580, Robert Persons met Thomas Tresham and changed his life. His Catholic faith came alive and he dared to stand up against Elizabeth's religious laws. This was exactly what alarmed the government. Over 100 new priests had arrived from Europe by 1580 and their work meant recusancy was increasing.

William Allen and the Pope ordered the priests to concentrate their work on wealthy Catholic gentry who could influence other Catholics and whose educated sons might enter the priesthood. The priests travelled in disguise under false names, helped by Catholic tradesmen and servants. But as Campion said in November 1580:

> I cannot long escape the hands of the … enemies [who] have so many eyes, so many tongues, so many scouts and crafts.

Knowing that the local Justice of the Peace might search the house while priests were staying, many gentry families created secret hiding places called 'priest's holes'. Their visitors might have to hide for days in tiny spaces behind walls or below floorboards with very little food or water until the coast was clear.

▲ Baddesley Clinton manor house. This was the home of a Catholic gentry family in Elizabeth's time. It had at least three different priest's holes, one in a toilet.

Walsingham's spies

In 1580, Elizabeth's Secretary of State was Sir Francis Walsingham. He built up a remarkable network of spies and informers to learn about the plans and movements of Catholic priests. This was a murky world where it was hard to know who could truly be trusted. Here are a few details of just four of the hundreds of agents who acted as Walsingham's eyes and ears:

> **Reflect**
>
> Which of these four spies do you think was most valuable to Walsingham and Elizabeth's government?

Anthony Munday

The son of a London tradesman.

When in Rome, he pretended to be a Catholic and heard English priests planning to re-convert England. He told Walsingham what he knew.

Wrote a very influential anti-Catholic propaganda book that earned him lots of money and went on to be a successful poet and playwright.

William Parry

Son of a Welsh gentry family.

When he was deep in debt and needed money he offered to spy on Catholics abroad.

He seems to have joined the Catholic side as a double agent. In 1585 he was caught plotting to kill the Queen but claimed this was a ruse to impress the Catholics.

He was tried as a traitor and executed.

Charles Sledd

From a humble background.

Working as a servant for a Catholic Englishman in Rome, he overheard plans to kill the Queen. He passed these plans on in great detail in a file that named over 300 disloyal English Catholics.

Sledd seems to have acted from a genuine desire to keep England Protestant.

George Eliot

Worked as the steward for a Catholic gentry family in England. He committed a murder and went to the Earl of Leicester for help.

In return for a royal pardon, he passed on secrets about Catholic gentry families who hid priests. Eliot became a full-time *poursuivant* (priest-catcher). Catholics called him Judas Eliot.

The mission of Edmund Campion, 1580-81: a case study

Campion's story reveals the difficulties faced by the English Catholic priests.

Capture

After months of travelling in disguise between gentry houses, Campion was captured in July 1581 at Lyford Grange in Oxfordshire. George Eliot, the priest-catcher, arrived at the house, probably acting on a tip-off. Eliot needed two days and many assistants to find Campion and three other priests hiding in a hollow space behind a wall. All four were taken to London to be tried.

In August 1580, a pamphlet written by Campion was printed and distributed by Catholics from a secret printing press in Oxfordshire. In it he said he had come

> to preach the Gospel (and) to give a spiritual warning against the foul vice and proud ignorance by which many of my dear countrymen are abused. I never intended, and am strictly forbidden by the Pope who sent me, to deal with matters of state or policy of this realm. They have nothing to do with my work.

In his own mind, Campion was a loyal Englishman who simply believed that Elizabeth was wrong about religion. To Elizabeth and her government he could not be loyal if he opposed her supremacy over the Church and took orders from the Pope. Religion and politics could not be separated: he was a traitor.

> **Reflect**
> 1. Why would the government have been angry that the Catholics had their own printing presses?
> 2. Do these words of Campion's prove that he really was a loyal subject of Queen Elizabeth?

Torture and trial

Campion was tortured on the rack, a machine that slowly stretched his arms and legs out of joint. He revealed the names of Catholics who had helped him. One was Thomas Tresham, which explains why he and others were arrested. (See page 28.) But, even under torture, Campion insisted that he never encouraged rebellion against Elizabeth.

At his trial in November 1581, the only witnesses who swore that they had heard Campion call on Catholics to rebel against their Queen were the government's own spies Andrew Munday, George Eliot and Charles Sledd. Despite this he was found guilty of treason and condemned to death.

Execution

On 1 December 1581, Campion and two other priests were dragged by horses to their place of execution at Tyburn in London. His captors told him to beg for the Queen's forgiveness. Campion said he had no need of forgiveness from Elizabeth as he had done her no wrong. He prayed that she should have a long and prosperous reign.

Religious heretics would be burned alive, but the priests were executed as traitors, that is they were hanged and taken down to be cut open while still conscious. Their internal organs were burned in front of them and in front of a large crowd. Parts of their body were then put on public display to deter anyone from following their example.

▲ This is another Catholic propaganda image from 1584. It shows the different stages in the hanging, drawing and quartering of Campion and the other priests in December 1581. It creates a much more brutal impression than is suggested by the painting at the start of the enquiry on page 26. In that image, Campion is shown to the left of centre wearing a blue cloak.

Why were there so few Catholics in Elizabeth's kingdom by 1603?

Propaganda and persistence, 1581–95

Robert Persons managed to leave England in 1581 without being captured. So did another English Catholic called Richard Rowlande, who had dared to publish a short account of Campion's death that accused Elizabeth of murdering Campion for his beliefs rather than for any act of treason. In 1587, Rowlande (using his Dutch grandfather's name of Verstegan) published books that claimed to show how Elizabeth treated Catholics. The images on page 30 and 31 are taken from his book. Torture was used far more under Elizabeth than any other English monarch and Rowlande particularly criticised her chief torturer, Richard Topcliffe, a deeply sadistic man who sometimes tortured prisoners in his home.

Elizabeth's government countered this Catholic propaganda by publishing books that gave its own viewpoint. It even wrote a pamphlet to justify its use of torture.

Robert Persons and William Allen became more extreme in their opposition to Elizabeth after the death of Campion. They sent many more priests to England. In 1585, Elizabeth's Act against Priests (see page 30) said that any priest ordained under the authority of the Pope was guilty of treason just for setting foot in England. If caught, the priests were sure to be executed. But they still came.

The 'Bloody Question'

When put on trial after 1585, priests always had to answer what became known as the 'Bloody Question'. This asked them whose side they would take if a foreign power were to obey the Pope and invade England to remove Elizabeth from the throne. If they replied that they would support Elizabeth, their credibility as a priest was gone. If they declared their support for the Pope, they had shown themselves to be traitors.

As the graph shows, most priests were executed in the late 1580s. This was the time, as you will see later, when England was most at risk of an actual invasion by Spanish forces acting with the Pope's blessing.

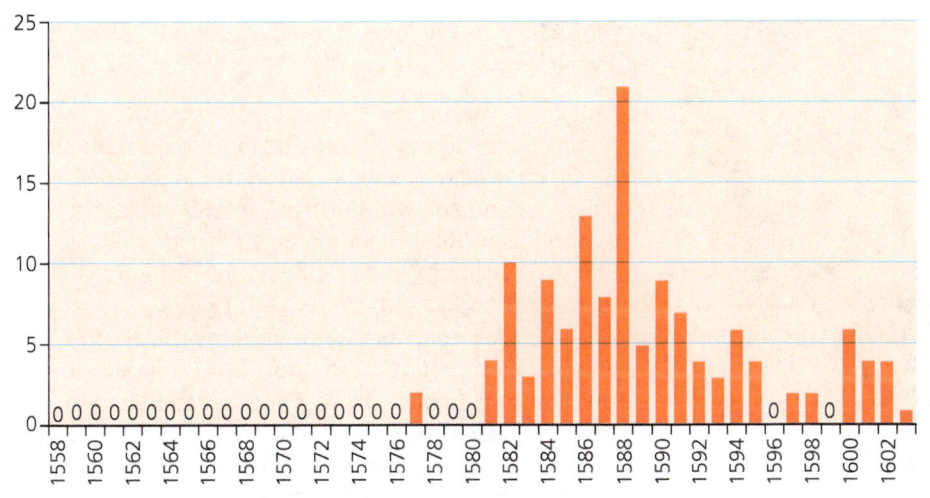

◀ Number of Catholic priests who were either executed or died in prison during the reign of Elizabeth I

> ### Reflect
> Why do you think there were so many executions and deaths of priests after 1585?

Final years of failure, 1596–1603

The number of Catholic priests in England rose again towards the end of Elizabeth's reign when it was clear that she would soon die, but they achieved very little. Their attempts to rebuild the Catholic faith in their homeland had failed by 1603. Historians give different reasons for this:

- Some say the priests failed because they did not concentrate their work in the north and west where recusancy was strongest. They spent too much time near London and failed to build a strong base.
- Some say the priests concentrated their work on the gentry, neglecting lower-class Catholics who then became Protestants.
- Others say that priests like Campion were too saintly to have a realistic chance of overcoming the weight of Elizabeth's government's power. Whether they liked it or not, they were involved in a political struggle.
- Some say the seminary priests and the Jesuits spent too much time squabbling over what they should try to do. The seminary priests said they should simply support existing Catholics while Jesuits were more radical and wanted to convert Protestants. In 1598, the Pope appointed a special Archpriest to decide on how to support English Catholics but the two groups argued about him as well. As they bickered, their threat to Elizabeth declined and so did the number of English Catholics.

> ### Record
> Complete your timeline explanation chart on 'The work of English priests, 1580–1603'.

Record

On a new sheet of paper, start making your final explanation chart as described on page 27. Use the section heading 'International affairs: the Scottish queen and the Spanish king'.

International affairs – the Scottish queen and the Spanish king, 1580–1603

By now you will have realised that the experiences of Catholics in England were greatly affected by the arrival of priests who had been trained overseas. In this section you will see how the world of international politics also added to the pressures on English Catholics, whether they liked it or not. At the centre of the story is one woman: Mary Queen of Scots.

Mary Queen of Scots – a dangerous cousin

There were two queens in England in 1580. One was Queen Elizabeth and the other was her cousin Mary Queen of Scots. Mary had fled from Scotland to England in 1568 after powerful Protestant lords rose up against her Roman Catholic rule. Instead of helping her cousin to regain her throne, Elizabeth kept her prisoner. She did not want to start a war with Scotland. Besides, Mary had ruled badly and was accused of murdering her own husband, so there were good reasons for not sending her back. But the decision to keep Mary in England created all sorts of problems:

1. Mary was directly descended from the first Tudor King, Henry VII. If Elizabeth died without children, Mary was next in line to the English throne – and she would turn England back to Catholicism. Keeping Mary in England gave English Catholics hope and encouragement.
2. Almost as soon as Mary arrived, English Catholics started causing trouble for Elizabeth. A Catholic rebellion in the north of England was put down in 1569 and a plot to murder Elizabeth was discovered in 1571. Even if Mary had no direct part in planning these, her presence as a figurehead for revolt was stirring trouble from English Catholics in ways that Elizabeth had been able to avoid until her cousin arrived.
3. Mary's presence in England as a ready-made Catholic replacement for the Protestant Queen Elizabeth led the Pope to excommunicate Elizabeth in 1570. He ordered English Catholics to disobey her laws. As you learned on page 32, this led to a new wave of English Catholic priests working secretly in England, strengthening Catholic resistance. This then led to increases in recusancy fines.

By 1580, Mary had been living in fairly comfortable captivity in England for twelve years. She refused to allow any English court to put her on trial for the murder of her husband in Scotland. Elizabeth used this fact to justify keeping her cousin in captivity. This turned some English Catholics against their own queen and a few were drawn into plots to release Mary. Her presence meant all English Catholics were under suspicion. This is why Walsingham's spies kept them and Mary under such close observation, especially after 1580 when Pope Gregory XIII announced that it was not a sin for a Catholic to murder Elizabeth.

▲ Mary Queen of Scots. A miniature portrait by Nicholas Hilliard, 1578

Reflect

What made Mary's presence in England such a threat to Elizabeth?

Why were there so few Catholics in Elizabeth's kingdom by 1603?

The Throckmorton Plot, 1583

In 1583, Walsingham's spies told him that the Jesuit Robert Persons had recruited a young English Catholic, Francis Throckmorton, into a plot against Elizabeth. Throckmorton was arrested and tortured. He confessed to working with the Duke of Guise, a powerful French Catholic who was a relative of Mary Queen of Scots. The Duke was planning to invade England and put Mary on the throne, with support from the Pope and the Spanish king, Philip II.

Throckmorton was executed but Mary was safe: there was no proof that she had set up the plan. William Cecil persuaded a reluctant Elizabeth to let Parliament pass a Bond of Association. This said that anyone plotting to kill Elizabeth should be hunted down and executed and so should any person 'for whom such a detestable act shall be attempted'. In other words, Mary could be executed even if she knew nothing about a plot to put her on the throne.

Reflect

1. At first, Robert Persons steered clear of plotting against Elizabeth. What changed his mind?
2. How was the Bond of Association supposed to reduce the threat to Elizabeth I?

Mary's trial and execution

On 12 October 1586, Mary was put on trial at Fotheringhay Castle in Northamptonshire. She skilfully fought her own case, arguing that:

- God had made her a queen and no court had the right to try her. (Elizabeth secretly agreed.)
- No original messages existed. Evidence could have been forged. (Some was.)
- Babington, Ballard and others gave their evidence against her under torture.

Mary was found guilty. Elizabeth refused to sign a warrant for Mary's death for several weeks. She hated the idea of killing another queen. When she eventually did sign the warrant, William Cecil immediately sent it to Fotheringhay. Mary was executed on 8 February 1587. Elizabeth was furious. She said she never gave the order to send the warrant and was innocent of her cousin's death, but many historians think Elizabeth knew exactly what she was doing.

The Babington Plot, 1586

By 1586, Mary's presence in England meant that Walsingham had agents all over England and around Europe looking for the slightest sign of danger to Elizabeth. It is no wonder that Catholics in England felt under pressure to give up their faith. One careless word might lead to prison or execution.

In July of that year, a rich young Catholic, Anthony Babington, met a Jesuit priest called John Ballard. Ballard persuaded Babington to join a plot to kill Elizabeth and place Mary on the English throne. Babington found what he thought was a safe way of communicating secretly with Mary. He placed coded letters inside waterproof tubes and hid them in beer barrels that went in and out of the house in Staffordshire where she was then being held.

Ballard and Babington had no idea that one of Walsingham's cleverest spies, Thomas Phelippes, knew all about their secret messages. He intercepted them all, broke the codes and made copies before sending the original messages on. In early August, Babington and Ballard were arrested and, under torture, they confirmed that Mary had agreed to the plan. In September they were executed.

Reflect

In the image below, the artist shows Mary Queen of Scots as a brave, proud woman arguing her case at her trial.

How does he achieve this?

▼ Mary Queen of Scots defends herself during her trial. From a history book published in 1920

▲ The 'Armada Portrait' of Elizabeth I, c.1588

The impact of international politics

This famous image of Queen Elizabeth I shows her as a world leader: one hand rests on a globe and the other on a sword, the crown of an emperor sits next to her and the mermaid carved onto the arm of the chair suggests her power over the seas. Behind her, two paintings show the arrival and the destruction of the Spanish Armada in 1588. But although she looks confident here, England was never really secure in international affairs at any point during her reign.

Roots of rivalry with Spain

England was a Protestant nation but Europe's two great powers, France and Spain, were Catholic. By 1580, France was divided and distracted by her own struggles between the ruling Catholics and the Protestants. Meanwhile, England and Spain were quickly becoming serious enemies. There were several reasons for this:

- Elizabeth I had refused to marry Philip II of Spain at the start of her reign.
- Throughout the 1570s, English sailors such as Drake and Hawkins acted like pirates, attacking Spanish ports and ships in the 'New World'.
- Spain ruled the Netherlands and Philip II was angry when Elizabeth sent money to aid Protestant Dutch rebels there in the 1570s.
- Philip II was a deeply religious Catholic and in 1580, when Pope Gregory said that it would not be a sin to kill Elizabeth, Philip started to support plotters who wanted to replace her with Mary Queen of Scots.

> **Reflect**
>
> Why might England's bad relations with Spain have made Elizabeth more worried about a threat from English Catholics?

The Anglo-Spanish war begins, 1585

In 1584, a Catholic subject of Philip II shot and killed the leader of the Dutch Protestant rebels, Prince William of Orange. The murder shocked Elizabeth. She knew the same could happen to her.

Elizabeth's advisers had been trying to get her to send an army to help the Dutch rebels for many years and after this murder she finally decided to do so. In 1585, she signed a treaty with the Dutch rebels and sent the Earl of Leicester with an army of 7,000 men to fight against the Spanish in the Netherlands. England and Spain were at war.

Despite Leicester's poor leadership, the English troops did stop Spanish advances in the Netherlands. At the same time, Francis Drake sailed to the Caribbean (then known as the West Indies) and attacked Spanish ports there and returned with treasure from Spanish ships.

▲ Gold coin showing Philip II of Spain, 1557

The Spanish Armada, 1588

In Spain, Philip II decided to launch a crusade: medieval knights had obeyed the Pope by fighting Muslim 'unbelievers' in the Holy Land, and his Catholic army would serve the Pope by invading England and defeating its Protestant heretics.

He started to build an armada, an enormous fleet of ships. It was to sail from Spain to the Netherlands and collect an army of 20,000 troops led by Philip's best general, the Duke of Parma. The Armada would then carry his army to England.

A surprise attack by Francis Drake on the Spanish port of Cadiz in 1587 damaged many of the Armada's ships and delayed its sailing by months. This, and the execution of Mary Queen of Scots in that same year, made Philip even more determined to succeed. By July 1588, his great Armada was ready to sail.

In England, the government's campaign to catch Catholic priests reached new heights in 1588. You can see this by the graph on page 35. More recusants than ever were rounded up by Justices of the Peace and put in prison. These included those like Thomas Tresham who still insisted that they were loyal to Elizabeth. The government was determined to stop any English Catholics from leading a rising in support of an invading Spanish army.

In the end, Philip's army failed to land in England. His Armada was defeated by a mixture of bad planning, bad luck and skilful tactics from the English sailors and their Dutch allies. For example:

1. Philip put the Duke of Medina Sidonia in charge of the Armada, but he had little experience of sailing.
2. The Armada of 130 ships sailed up the English Channel chased by English ships. It waited at Calais for the Duke of Parma's army.
3. Dutch ships blocked the Duke of Parma's army in the Netherlands stopping it from joining up with the Armada.
4. The English set fire to some old ships and let them drift into the Armada as fireships. The Spanish panicked, cut their anchors and sailed north.
5. Near Gravelines, the English ships attacked the Spanish. One Spanish ship sank. The Spanish guns were unreliable but the English ones worked well. 1,000 Spanish men died and only 50 English were killed.
6. The Armada was driven north by the winds and headed back to Spain by sailing north around Scotland.
7. Powerful storms wrecked about 44 Spanish ships off Scotland and Ireland. About 80 ships eventually struggled back to Spain.

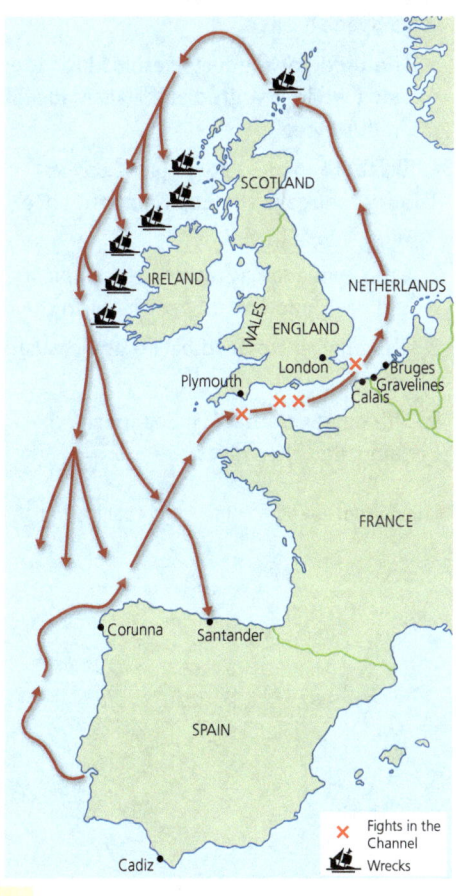

▲ A map of western Europe in the 1580s showing route of the Spanish Armada

Reflect

Which do you think did most to cause the failure of the Armada:

- bad luck
- bad planning
- skilful tactics shown by the English and Dutch?

Myths about the Armada

The story of the Armada's defeat has been passed down over the years. The version that most people know is often full of myths such as:

> **Reflect**
>
> Why do you think myths like these last so long?

The myth	What most historians say
1. The English calmly waited for the Armada to arrive – Drake finished a game of bowls.	The English wanted to attack the Armada before it got into the English Channel, but the wind kept their ships in Plymouth.
2. Drake commanded the English fleet and brought England victory.	Lord Howard of Effingham was the commander.
3. The Armada heavily outnumbered the English fleet.	The Armada had many troop-carrier ships but each side had about 30–35 warships.
4. Smaller English ships pluckily defeated large Spanish ones.	The ships were about the same size, but the English ships changed direction more easily and had better guns.
5. The tactic of sending fireships into the Armada while it waited at Calais made all the difference.	If Dutch ships had not blocked the Duke of Parma's armies at Bruges, the Armada would have picked up the troops and would not have been anchored at Calais.
6. Elizabeth made a stirring speech at Tilbury that gave the English confidence.	Elizabeth made her speech days after the Armada cut its anchors and was driven north by the wind. It was near Scotland when Elizabeth made her speech!
7. If the Armada had succeeded, England would have become a Spanish colony.	Philip II did not want to rule England. He just wanted to restore the Catholic faith.
8. The English suffered barely any casualties.	Elizabeth kept the sailors on board ship for weeks after as she could not afford to pay them. Thousands died of hunger and disease.
9. The defeat of the Armada meant that Britain ruled the waves.	Britain only achieved control of the seas in the eighteenth century.

▼ Important episodes in the Anglo-Spanish War after 1588

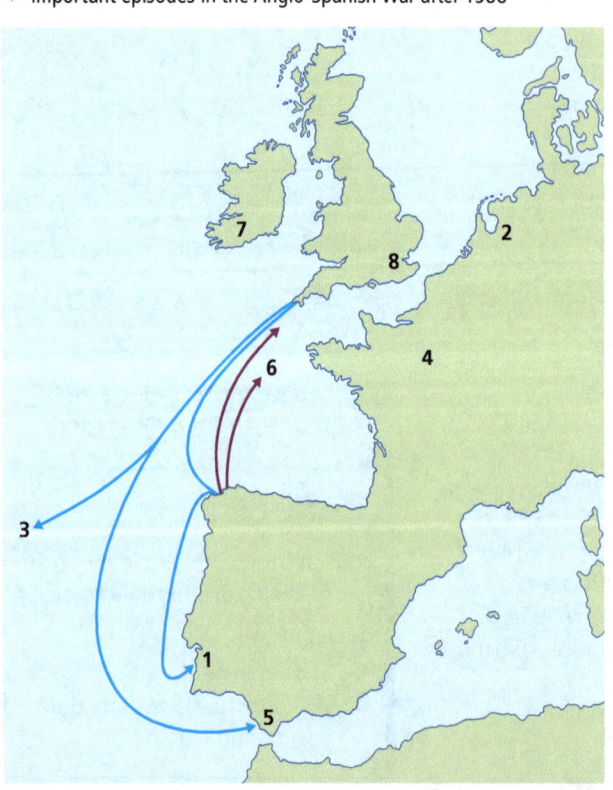

The war continues

The defeat of the 1588 Armada did not end England's war with Spain. It dragged on until 1604, a year after Elizabeth died. Here are some of the main events of those years.

1. 1589 – Francis Drake led an 'English Armada' to attack Portugal and stir the Portuguese to revolt against Spain. It was an expensive failure.
2. 1594 – The northern Netherlands became a secure Protestant area, virtually independent from Spain. Spain still ruled a weakened southern Netherlands but was much less likely to attack England.
3. 1595 – Francis Drake and John Hawkins died at sea while attempting to raid Spanish ships and ports in the 'New World'.
4. 1596 – England formed an alliance with France and with the Protestant Netherlands against Spain.
5. 1596 – The Earl of Essex led a successful raid on the Spanish port of Cadiz.
6. 1596 and 1597 – Philip II sent Spain's second and third Armadas against England – but both were wrecked by storms.
7. 1601 – A Spanish army landed in Ireland. The Earl of Tyrone had started a Catholic rebellion against English rule in 1594 and the Spanish hoped to help him win and create a base for an invasion of England. The Spanish force was defeated and Tyrone's rebellion finally ended in 1603.
8. 1604 – One year after Elizabeth's death, the war with Spain was ended by the Treaty of London. It had lasted almost twenty years.

Why were there so few Catholics in Elizabeth's kingdom by 1603?

England's Catholics by 1603

By 1603, when Elizabeth died, almost all England's Catholics had given up their faith or were attending Protestant church services each week without complaint. Philip II died in 1598 and his son Philip III was a weak ruler. Since the death of Mary Queen of Scots there was no obvious Catholic leader to replace Elizabeth. The heir to her throne was almost certainly Mary's son, James VI of Scotland, who was a Protestant. The English Catholics were under constant pressure from the state and from their neighbours to make them conform.

But a small core of English Catholics remained. In 1605, just two years after Elizabeth died, a few of these die-hards planned the famously unsuccessful Gunpowder Plot that aimed to assassinate King James and his government. One of the plotters was Francis Tresham. He was the son of Thomas, who you learned about at the start of this enquiry. Unlike his father, he obviously was a real threat to the monarch's safety. For the next two hundred years, English Catholics were sneered at as 'papists', treated as second-class citizens and were still suspected of being 'dangerous people'.

Record

Complete your timeline explanation chart on 'International affairs: the Scottish queen and the Spanish king'.

Review

1. Make a large version of this diagram with lots of space in each of the three segments.
2. Now study the three timeline explanation charts you have made. From each one, choose some really important events or developments that help to explain why there were so few Catholics in England by 1603. Write them into the relevant segment of the diagram.
3. Now draw lines to connect statements that you think are connected in some important way. For example, if you have written that 'In 1580 the Pope said it was not a sin to murder Elizabeth', you could connect that with 'Walsingham's spy network kept a very close watch on English Catholics'. On the line that you draw between events, write a simple explanation of **why** they are connected.
4. Now compare your finished diagram with ones that others have made. Decide why your diagrams may differ and whether you should change your diagram in any way.

And finally ...

5. You have been thinking mainly about why the number of English Roman Catholics fell so sharply between 1580 and 1603. This is, of course, very closely tied to the fact that Catholics were seen as a threat to Queen Elizabeth.

   Test how good your notes are by using them to plan answers to these two questions:

   a) When, if at all, do you think English Catholics posed a really serious threat to Elizabeth's rule?
   b) 'Elizabeth and her government over-reacted to the supposed "Catholic threat".' How far do you agree with this statement?

CLOSER LOOK 2

'Little John' and how he is remembered

This fine bronze monument is set into a niche in the wall at St Mary's Roman Catholic Church at Harvington in Worcestershire. It was made in 1825 to commemorate the life and work of a man named Nicholas Owen, known to many in his lifetime as 'Little John'. He was, apparently, really very short.

Owen was probably born in Oxford in 1562. He was from a quite humble background. His father, Walter, was a carpenter and in 1577 Nicholas started an apprenticeship to become a joiner. (This was a rather more skilful form of carpentry.) We do not know whether he was raised in a Catholic household or was converted by priests from abroad, but he clearly had a very deep faith. He became a Jesuit lay-brother, which means he swore the Jesuit oath of total commitment to God, but never trained as a priest.

By 1588, evidence in letters written by Jesuits show that he had blended his faith with his skills at working in wood and stone: he was building remarkably clever priest's holes in gentry houses all over England. He continued this work until 1606 when he was finally arrested after the Gunpowder Plot.

The monument

The monument shows Owen dressed in the clothes of an artisan (skilled worker) of his day. In his hand he holds his saw and his foot secures a plank on his workbench. Behind him in the lower part of the carving are:

- the horse that carried him all over England
- his bag of carpentry tools
- tree branches that provided his timber
- immediately above the tree branches is Hindlip Hall where he and two Jesuit priests were arrested in 1606.

To the left we see:

- a priest (or possibly Owen) kneeling in prayer in a priest's hole
- three prisoners being escorted up a hill by a guard.

At the top, behind him, we see the Tower of London where Owen died, almost certainly while he was being tortured on the rack, although the torturers claimed he killed himself. Some people say the object above the priest's hole represents the rack on which he died.

▲ Monument to Nicholas Owen at St Mary's Church, Harvington, c.1825

Statues, monuments and interpretations of history

Monuments, including statues of famous men and women all over Britain, are another way of passing on a particular interpretation of history. The person's character and achievements are always suggested by their posture and by the objects that are included.

In this case, there is nothing sinister or devious in Owen's appearance. He is portrayed as a humble, working man. This is not surprising as the monument is in a Catholic church and was placed there to honour Owen. You can also see him in the painting of English and Welsh martyrs on page 26. He is kneeling at the front with just a small, sharp knife in his belt to suggest his skills at working with wood.

Historic sites and interpretations

Very near to St Mary's Church is Harvington Hall. In the sixteenth century, this large Elizabethan country house was owned by a recusant family called the Pakingtons.

In 1580, Humphrey Pakington pulled down the fourteenth-century manor house that stood on the site and replaced it with this fine hall. It now belongs to the Roman Catholic Church.

Like many similar properties, Harvington Hall helps to pay for its upkeep through tourism. One of its attractions for tourists is that the house may have more priest's holes than any other property in Britain. Nicholas Owen probably made some or all of these. One is reached by a fake fireplace. After searching houses like this, priest-catchers used to stand outside and check whether all the fireplaces they had seen inside matched the position of the chimneys.

School groups have the opportunity to visit and to take part in events run by historical re-enactors who take the parts of people who lived and worked at the site in the past. Re-enactment is another form of historical interpretation. Some people find it a really helpful way of understanding how life was lived long ago. Others would prefer to let their own imagination do the work, guided by some carefully worded leaflets, display boards or perhaps an audio guide.

As with all historical interpretations, there is always the need to be true to the history and to avoid over-simplified or exaggerated versions of the past.

▲ A historical re-enactor emerges from a priest's hole at Harvington Hall, through a very narrow opening. The 'door' is a swivelling oak beam

Reflect

What factors may affect the strict historical accuracy of interpretations given in monuments and at historical sites?

▼ Harvington Hall, Worcestershire

3

Daily lives

What mattered to the Elizabethans?

This is an unusual picture. It tells the story of Sir Henry Unton, from his birth in 1558 to his death in 1596. The painting was commissioned by Dorothy Unton in memory of her dead husband. Sir Henry Unton stares out from the centre of the painting. Beneath him, you can see Sir Henry's funeral procession. A group of poor people are sitting under the trees, hoping that the mourners will give them alms as they pass by. On the left is Faringdon Church where Sir Henry Unton was buried. The artist shows us his memorial which stood inside the church. On the right are scenes which give us glimpses of Sir Henry Unton's life.

▼ A painting of the life and death of Sir Henry Unton by an unknown artist, c. 1596

Reflect

1. Start in the bottom right-hand corner, and find an interesting detail in each of the following scenes from Sir Henry Unton's life:
   a) as a baby in his mother's arms
   b) studying at Oxford University
   c) travelling in Italy during the 1570s
   d) serving as a soldier in the Netherlands
   e) on his way to France as Elizabeth I's ambassador
   f) on his deathbed in France, being treated by a doctor
   g) his body coming back to England on a ship with black sails
   h) enjoying life at Wadely, his home in Berkshire.
2. What can the painting tell us about the daily life of an Elizabethan gentleman like Sir Henry Unton?

What mattered to the Elizabethans?

The Enquiry

So far, your depth study of the Elizabethans has focused on politics and religion. These are important aspects of England's history in the years 1580–1603, but they are not the whole story. In the 1970s some historians became interested in the daily lives of Elizabethan people. They began to ask interesting questions, not just about the lives of rich men like Sir Henry Unton, but about the lives of labouring families and of the 'middling sort'. These social historians used historical documents that no one had thought to study before. They made some fascinating discoveries about the daily lives of the Elizabethans.

In this enquiry you will find out what the research of social historians has revealed about the daily lives of different Elizabethans. Your focus will be: **What mattered to the Elizabethans?** As you work through the enquiry you will do three things:

1. Compare the daily lives of rich, middling and poor Elizabethans.
2. Decide how far you think Elizabethan family life was different from today.
3. Explain how the Elizabethans tackled the problem of poverty.

The lives of rich, middling and poor Elizabethans

Record

The information on the following six pages will help you to compare the daily lives of rich, middling and poor Elizabethans. You will find out about:

- people's houses and possessions
- the food people ate
- other aspects of their lives.

Make a comparison chart like the one below and add points to it as you go along.

	Gentry	Middling sort	Labourers
Houses and possessions			
Food			
Other aspects			

▲ A portrait of Sir Edward Phelips, c.1604

Reflect

What impression did Sir Edward Phelips want to convey through his portrait? Think about: his face, his stance, his clothes, the setting, the objects in the portrait.

The gentry

This is a portrait of Sir Edward Phelips. Like Sir Henry Unton, Edward Phelips was an Elizabethan gentleman. The Phelips family were landowners who had lived in the village of Montacute in Somerset since the fifteenth century. Edward Phelips added to the family's wealth by becoming a successful lawyer. In the 1580s, he became a member of parliament and was later knighted by King James I. In 1604, Sir Edward Phelips was chosen as speaker of the House of Commons. The bag of office he is holding suggests that this portrait was painted around this time.

In 1587, Edward Phelips inherited his father's property in Montacute, and soon decided to build a new house that would truly reflect his wealth and status. Through the 1590s, builders, glaziers and carpenters created a magnificent new house for Edward Phelips. In 1601, it was finally finished. Today, it is hard to imagine the impact that new country houses like Montacute would have had on Elizabethan people. Montacute was a medium-sized country house with around twenty rooms, but the homes of the gentry sometimes had over 50 rooms. These huge houses were designed to reflect the wealth and status of their owners.

As visitors approached the front of Montacute House, they would have been impressed by its size and symmetry. They would have admired the huge glazed windows, the tall decorated chimneys, the beautiful curved gables at each end of the house. As visitors stepped into the house they would have noticed the Phelips' coat of arms carved above the entrance. For a closer look at Montacute House see page 47 and pages 60–61.

Food and feasting

Gentry houses like Montacute House were surrounded by gardens, orchards and estate farms which ensured that their owners always had a plentiful supply of food. The rich and varied diet of the Elizabethan gentry marked them out from the common people. This was most clearly demonstrated at a

What mattered to the Elizabethans?

▲ Montacute House, Somerset

feast. A feast in a gentleman's house could include: beef, pork, venison, goose, swan, pheasant and a wide range of small birds. A fish course of salmon, eel, cod, pickled herring and pike might also be served. (A pike alone would have cost 30 times the daily wage of an Elizabethan labourer.) The food was served with great ceremony. Up to twenty servants formed a long procession and carried the food on silver and pewter platters from the kitchen to the great chamber. A feast would start in the late morning and could last for two hours. Guests would drink a lot of fine wine imported from France and Italy. After the feast, there might be a banquet – a sweet course where people ate sugar and marzipan confections. Some gentlemen, like Edward Phelips, even built special banqueting houses in their gardens where guests could enjoy the sweets.

Land and power

The wealth of the Elizabethan gentry came from their ownership of land. Around two per cent of the population were gentlemen, but they owned over half the land in England. The rents from their estates meant that gentlemen did not have to do manual work. It was this which set the gentry apart from the rest of Elizabethan society. While a nobleman such as a duke, earl or baron might own tens of thousands of acres in different estates across England, a minor gentleman might own just one estate of a few hundred acres. But it was their ownership of land which united the gentry and which gave them such incredible wealth.

Ownership of land also gave the Elizabethan gentry political power. As Justices of the Peace they enforced the Queen's laws and as members of parliament they helped her to govern. Their ownership of land and their office-holding set the gentry apart from other Elizabethans, but the great divide between the gentry and the 'common people' could be crossed. In Elizabethan England, men who had made their money in the law or in trade could sometimes buy land and enjoy the wealth, status and power of an Elizabethan gentleman.

Reflect

How did Montacute House reflect the wealth and status of Sir Edward Phelips?

Record

Complete the 'Gentry' section of your comparison chart. Under 'Other aspects' you could include information about land ownership, servants and office-holding.

The 'middling sort'

When they described their society, Elizabethans often spoke of 'gentlemen', 'the middling sort of people' and 'the poor'. In the towns, the middling sort were the independent tradesmen and craftsmen who owned their own businesses. These men were poorer than the wealthy merchants who ruled the town, but much richer than the labourers who made up half of the town's population.

In the countryside, middling people were the yeomen and husbandmen who farmed some land of their own. These families were nowhere near as wealthy as the gentry, but their daily lives were more comfortable than those of the labouring poor. Husbandmen were small farmers who usually rented a farm of between 5 and 50 acres. Yeomen were bigger farmers who often owned more than 50 acres of land and who employed farm labourers. Elizabethan yeoman were not important enough to become members of parliament or Justices of the Peace, but they often ruled their villages by becoming churchwardens or overseers of the poor.

Houses

▼ Pendean – a yeoman's house from West Lavington, West Sussex

This is a small yeoman's house from the south of England. It was built by a yeoman farmer called Richard Clare at the beginning of the seventeenth century. The house has been carefully reconstructed at an open-air museum. Richard Clare's new house was a big improvement on yeomen's houses from earlier times. You can see that it is well built with a strong oak frame, and both upstairs and downstairs rooms. Richard built a massive chimney in his new house and included fireplaces in both his downstairs rooms. Chimneys transformed the houses of middling people. For the first time, houses could be divided with ceilings as the smoke no longer had to find its way out through the rafters. If you look closely, you can see that Richard Clare also included another new feature in his house – glass windows! These made the houses of the middling sort lighter and less draughty. With upstairs rooms, chimneys and glass windows, the houses of the Elizabethan middling sort became much more comfortable.

> **Reflect**
>
> What new features did this yeoman's house contain?

Historians have discovered a huge amount about the houses of the yeomen, husbandmen, tradesman and craftsmen from probate inventories. These documents listed someone's possessions after they died. Some probate inventories included the names of different rooms and therefore provide fascinating glimpses into the daily lives of the middling sort. A yeoman's house usually had between five and ten rooms. Typical rooms were:

The hall. This was the main living and eating room of the house. Many yeomen's houses had no separate kitchen so the housewife cooked on the fire in the hall. The family ate at a long table and sat on wooden chairs, stools and benches. An oak cupboard held the pewter mugs, bowls and platters which had replaced the wooden tableware of earlier times.

The parlour. This was a living and sleeping room next to the hall. It contained the best bed belonging to the yeoman and his wife. The 'middling sort' could often afford feather mattresses and many parlours contained oak chests full of linen sheets and pillowcases.

Chambers. These rooms on the second floor of the house were where the children and servants slept. Chambers were also sometimes used for storing farm equipment and for smoking meat.

Service rooms. These might be attached to the house or built separately. They could include a kitchen, brew-house, bake-house and dairy. Middling families might have one or two female servants to prepare and cook their food, but the yeoman's wife would do much of the work herself.

> ## Reflect
> In what ways were houses of the Elizabethan middling sort quite comfortable? In what ways were they less impressive than the houses of the gentry?

Food

Middling families could afford to eat well, but their mealtimes had none of the ceremony found in gentry houses. They served their own food and their servants usually joined them at the table. The yeoman's farm provided beef, mutton and pork, but middling families did not eat the exotic meats enjoyed by the gentry. Bread was an important part of their diet but the best white flour would be saved for cakes and pastry when there were guests. Usually, middling people would eat 'yeoman bread' made of wheat flour with some of the bran left in. The gardens and orchards of the middling sort provided a variety of fruit and vegetables, but they could not afford luxuries like grapes or the new exotic vegetables that the gentry could buy. The middling sort drank beer and mead – their incomes would not stretch to the wines enjoyed by the gentry.

◀ A reconstruction of the interior of a house belonging to a middling Elizabethan family

> ## Reflect
> Which room has been reconstructed here? What can we learn from the reconstruction about the daily lives of the middling sort?

> ## Record
> Complete the 'middling sort' section of your comparison chart.

The labouring poor

The labouring poor made up about half the population of Elizabethan England, but historians find it difficult to find out about their daily lives because labourers did not leave many written records. Only wealthier labourers would have had probate inventories after their death. There are very few pictures of the labouring poor in Elizabethan England but this rare sketch below of a carter and porter in Elizabethan London, made by a foreign visitor, gives us a glimpse of how ordinary workers dressed and the kind of work that some of them did.

Unlike the two men in the picture, most Elizabethan labourers earned their living in the countryside. They worked on the farms of yeomen and husbandmen, starting at first light and working until dusk. Few labourers were lucky enough to be employed on a farm throughout the year. Most were day labourers who went from farm to farm looking for work. At harvest and haymaking time many farmers needed labourers, but at other times of year it could be hard for a labourer to find a day's work. When they had no wages, labouring families struggled to pay their rent, and to buy food and fuel.

More fortunate labourers might have an acre or two of land of their own, or they might enjoy common rights which allowed them to graze a couple of cows or a few sheep on the common land in the village. However, two-thirds of Elizabethan labourers only had their cottages and garden plots. Some poor labourers built themselves cottages (like the one opposite) on wasteland or on the edge of commons. However, an Act of 1589 tried to stop this by stating that all new cottages had to have at least four acres of land.

▶ A carter and porter in Elizabethan London

> **Reflect**
>
> What can this picture tell us about the lives of the labouring poor?

What mattered to the Elizabethans?

▲ A reconstruction of a labourer's cottage

Houses

Compared with the houses of the middling sort, labourers' cottages were small and poorly built. There were no upper rooms and no chimneys. The smoke from the fire escaped through the thatch. There was no glass in the windows and the small window openings made the houses very dark inside. Often, a labourer's house had just two rooms, each with a bare earth floor. There might be nothing in the hall apart from a table, bench and some wooden bowls, platters and spoons. The chamber might contain a wooden bed with a mattresses stuffed with straw.

Food

Bread was the main food of the labouring poor. This was mostly made from rye or barley as wheat was often too expensive. Pottage, a thick soup made from the vegetables grown in the garden, often simmered in cauldrons over labourers' fires. When times were good, there might be eggs, cheese, fish or bacon, and beer might be drunk. But when the harvests were poor, and the price of bread rose dramatically, poor labourers were often unable to feed their families. The wet summer of 1594 ruined the harvest, grain prices soared and the stomachs of labouring people in many parts of England began to ache with hunger. When the harvests of 1595 and 1596 also failed, some labouring people starved to death.

Reflect

This house was used in a documentary programme about the Elizabethans.

In what way was it a typical labourer's cottage?

Record

Complete the 'labouring poor' section of your comparison chart.

You might find it helpful to produce a visual version of your chart using little pictures to capture the main points.

Use your chart to explain what mattered to each of the three main groups in Elizabethan society.

Family life

This family portrait from 1567 shows Lord Cobham, his wife Frances (on the right) and their six children. On the left, the youngest child, Henry, is sitting on his aunt's lap. His brother Maximillian sits at the end of the table and ignores the puppy jumping up at him. William, the oldest son, is positioned close to his father. The twins, Elizabeth and Frances, and their younger sister, Margaret, sit in front of their mother.

The Cobhams had produced six children in just seven years. It was a 'fruitful' marriage and this is reflected in the silver plates of fruit on the table. The painting also contains some messages about the upbringing of children in Elizabethan England. Like the monkey and the puppy, children were playful, but they had to learn to control their behaviour. The parrot suggests that children should copy the behaviour of adults.

In many ways the Cobham family appears strange to modern eyes. Lord Cobham looks very severe and seems distant from his wife. Lord and Lady Cobham do not seem to enjoy being with their charming children. To us, relationships in the Cobham family appear formal, distant and cold. Of course, these impressions might be more to do with the conventions of Elizabethan painting than the reality of family life. We need to find out more ...

◀ A portrait of Lord Cobham and his family

> **Reflect**
>
> What interesting things do you notice about the portrait?

New research

In the 1970s, social historians began to ask interesting questions about family life in early modern England. They used sources such as diaries, parish registers, tax records, wills and criminal court records. These documents provided a fuller picture of family life, particularly among the middling people and labouring poor. As you will discover on the next three pages, their research has shown that although there were some interesting differences between family life in Elizabethan times and now, there were also some important similarities.

> **Record**
>
> Over the next three pages, you can read answers to some of the interesting questions which historians have asked about Elizabethan families. You will find out what historians have discovered about three aspects of family life:
>
> 1. husbands and wives
> 2. parents and children
> 3. the wider family.
>
> As you find out about each aspect, make two lists (Similarities and Differences) to compare Elizabethan family life with today.

Husbands and wives

How old were people when they married?

Men were usually in their late-twenties, and women in their mid-twenties when they married. Historians were surprised when they discovered that the Elizabethans married late, just like people do today. Most newly married couples set up in their own home, so they needed to save up before they could get married. However, in noble and gentry families, couples did not need to save so they often married much younger.

Did people have sex before they married?

No ... and yes. Single women sometimes gave birth to children, but illegitimate babies were quite uncommon. You might find this surprising, particularly as the Elizabethans did not have modern forms of contraception. But remember that sex outside marriage was forbidden by the Church. Many babies were baptised in the months following their parents' wedding. Up to 30 per cent of Elizabethan brides were pregnant when they married. It seems that many couples started having sex once they had decided to marry or were encouraged to marry once a pregnancy was discovered.

Were people free to choose who they married?

This depended on who you were. In gentry families, where property and status mattered, marriage was too important to be left to the young people themselves. Wealthy parents would expect to have a say in their child's choice of marriage partner, although this rarely went as far as arranging a marriage. Middling parents sometimes gave land, money and furniture to their children when they married, so parental approval could be important. Overall, however, it seems that most young people from middling and labouring families were free to marry whoever they wished. Unlike today, same-sex marriage was unknown in Elizabethan England.

How equal were husbands and wives?

Elizabethan wives were expected to obey their husbands at all times. At the same time, husbands were advised to respect their wives and to seek their advice. Women from the middling sort often helped to run family farms and workshops. Wives were certainly not afraid to quarrel with their husbands but Elizabethans disapproved of violent husbands and of scolding, domineering wives. The ideal was to avoid both of these extremes in a marriage.

Did marriages last?

When marriages broke down, there was little chance of a divorce in Elizabethan England. The breakdown of marriage could lead to informal separations, but a divorce required a private Act of Parliament. On the other hand, broken families were very common because of the early death of a husband or wife. When this occurred people usually remarried quite quickly. As today, many children in Elizabethan England were brought up by step-parents.

▼ 'A Skimmington Ride', a plaster frieze from Montacute House Somerset, early seventeenth century. This plaster frieze of a 'Skimmington' in the Great Hall of Montacute House shows what could happen when Elizabethan villagers disapproved of a married couple's behaviour. On the left a wife beats her husband with a shoe because he has been drinking beer while looking after the baby. On the right neighbours are ridiculing the man by carrying him round the village on a pole. An Elizabethan man was not expected to be violent, but he should not have allowed himself to be beaten by his wife!

Parents and children

◀ A portrait of Barbara Sidney and her six children

© By kind permission of Viscount De L'Isle from his private collection at Penshurst Place, Kent, England

> **Reflect**
>
> What can this portrait tell us about what mattered to Elizabethan noble families?

This painting, from 1596, shows Barbara Sidney with six of her children. The portrait was probably commissioned by Barbara's husband, Robert Sidney, Earl of Leicester. Before Barbara's death in 1621, the couple produced a total of eleven children. To us, all the children look like girls, but the two children with their mother's hand resting on them are in fact boys.

Only the wealthiest families have left portraits of their children, but social historians have used a range of other sources to answer questions about parents and children in Elizabethan England.

Were large families common?

No. It was usually only the nobility and gentry who had large families. Most Elizabethan families were quite small. In an age without efficient contraception, people inevitably produced lots of children, but children's lives were often very short. Standards of hygiene, safety and medical treatment were much lower in Elizabethan times than today, so many children died at an early age. Around a quarter of all children died before the age of ten.

How did parents treat their young children?

Some gentry families used 'wet nurses' to care for and breastfeed their infants, but most Elizabethan women looked after their own children. Historians used to think that parents did not invest too much love in their children because they knew that their little ones might die at an early age. However we now know that most Elizabethan parents formed strong emotional bonds with their children. Parents showed concern when children were ill, grief when they died and pride in their children's achievements.

What was family life like for older children?

From about the age of seven, parents with enough money sent their sons to school. In poorer families, children started to do some work at home or on the farm. They might be expected to gather wood, scare birds, mind babies or help at harvest time. At the age of twelve or thirteen, most boys left home to become apprentices or to work as farm servants. Girls, too, left their family homes to work as servants in the houses of other families. Up to a third of all families in Elizabethan England contained young people working as servants. From their early teens until they married in their twenties, most young people lived with someone else's family, gaining skills which would prepare them for adult life.

Were Elizabethan parents strict?

Elizabethan children were expected to obey their parents, but this did not always happen. Historians have discovered that children sometimes ignored their parents' wishes and were not always respectful. Arguments between fathers and sons seem to have been quite common. Physical punishment was much more widespread in Elizabethan England than today and beating was common in grammar schools. In the home, however, historians have found little evidence of harsh discipline and physical punishment. There is no evidence that cruelty towards children was more widespread in Elizabethan England than it is today.

Kinship (wider family)

Nowadays, there is a lot of flexibility in people's relationships with their wider family. Most people do not share a house with grandparents, aunts, uncles and cousins, although this sometimes occurs. Wider family members might live locally, but they are often scattered across the country and sometimes live abroad. Some people may have strong links with their wider relatives, others might never see their more distant kin. When historians first began to ask interesting questions about kinship in Elizabethan England, they expected to discover that the wider family was much more important to people then than it is today. In fact, their research revealed something quite different ...

Did people live with their wider family?

No. When historians started to analyse surviving listings of people living in Elizabethan communities, they were surprised to discover that households rarely included other kin outside the nuclear family of parents and children. The big houses of the gentry sometimes contained wider family members, but most people did not have members of their extended family living with them. When wider family members did live together in one house, it was usually the result of taking in someone who could not care for themselves, such as an elderly parent or an orphaned child. So, it seems that the structure of Elizabethan families was very similar to our own.

Did kin live in the same village?

No. Historians who analysed parish registers from different Elizabethan communities discovered that relatively few people had wider relatives living in the same village. You already know that in Elizabethan times most young people left home in their early teens to work as servants. It seems that they often married and settled in a different place. This meant that Elizabethan families were scattered, although it is likely that more people would have had relatives in nearby villages and towns. Unlike today, few Elizabethan people had relatives living abroad.

Did the wider family matter to people?

Yes and no. The gentry often showed a strong interest in their wider family and some middling families also had close links with their wider kin. Some historians think that in the north of England, where communities were more scattered, kinship mattered to people. In general however, kinship does not seem to have been particularly strong in Elizabethan England. When people wrote their wills, they focused on their own immediate family rather than their more distant relatives. In people's daily lives it was neighbours who mattered more than kin. When Elizabethan people attended church, drank in the alehouse and played rough football, it was neighbours rather than wider family they met. If they needed to borrow money, they were just as likely to turn to a neighbour as to a distant relative.

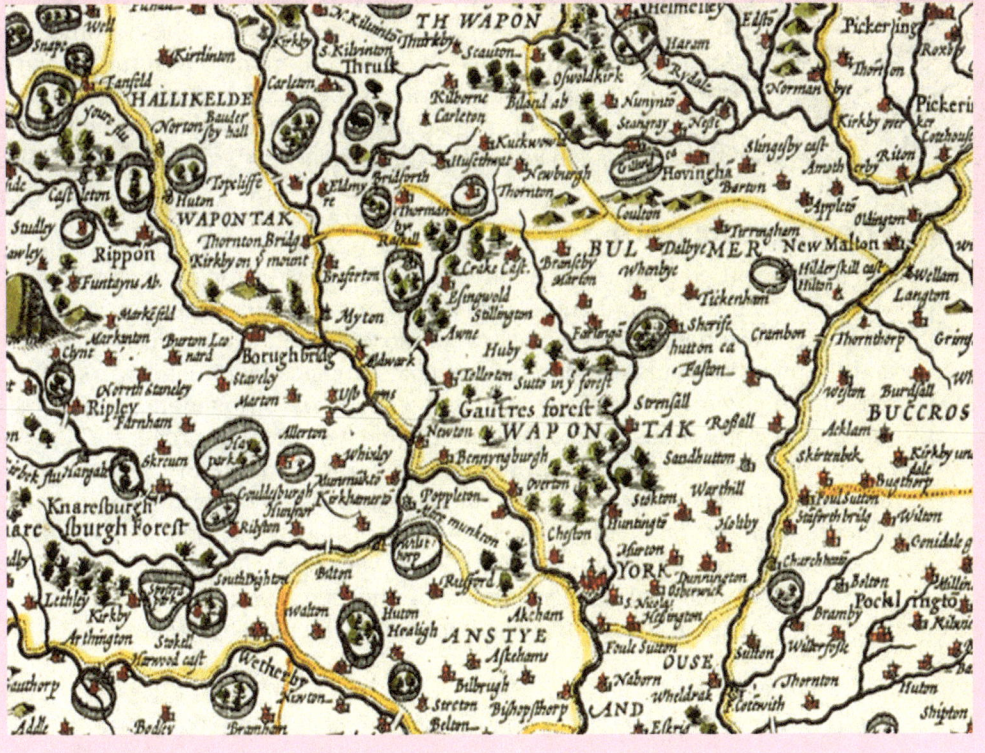

◀ A detail from John Speed's map of Yorkshire, 1611. Elizabethan people often had wider kin who had settled in different towns and villages.

The problem of poverty

Poverty was nothing new in Elizabethan England. There had always been people without enough money for adequate food, clothing and shelter. Yet the late sixteenth century saw a growth in poverty which was far worse than anything known before. In earlier periods, poverty had not been a major social problem. People had been poor usually as a result of a particular misfortune – the death of a spouse, sickness, injury – or because they were old and could no longer work. But by the end of the sixteenth century, the poor were not just victims of bad luck or old age. A large and growing proportion of the population lived in constant danger of falling into poverty. Many of these people were working labourers.

▼ A woodcut of a vagrant family from the late sixteenth century

The settled poor

In the last decades of Elizabeth's reign, English towns contained a shocking number of people living in poverty. In some places, these people, the settled poor, made up 30 per cent of the urban population. Many of the settled poor were children below the age of sixteen. Their chances of surviving into adulthood were slim. Poor children did not have enough to eat and often suffered from illness. They stood little chance of becoming an apprentice or a servant. Another large group among the settled poor were women who had been abandoned by their husbands. Typical of these was Alice Reade, aged 40 from Norwich, whose husband had left her with three children and a baby. Alice rented a room and earned a little money by spinning yarn. Her nine-year-old son and fourteen-year-old daughter also helped the family to survive by spinning. By far the largest group among the settled poor were older people, particularly widows. These women often tried to make a little money by spinning yarn, washing clothes or by begging on the streets. At times of plague, they sometimes even risked taking a job as a carer for people who were sick and dying.

The vagrant poor

Life for the settled poor was dismal, but at least these people usually had a room in which to live and could earn a little money or receive alms. Outside the towns were poor people who faced a more desperate situation – the vagrant poor. Vagrants wandered from place to place looking for work. They were usually young unmarried men and women travelling alone or in twos and threes. Sometimes, whole families could be seen on the road. If they were lucky, vagrants might find some seasonal work. More often, they were hustled on their way by fearful and suspicious villagers. Vagrants who were reluctant to move on were whipped out of parishes by local constables. All too often on winter mornings, the bodies of vagrants who had died of cold and hunger were found in barns and under hedges. Their burials, like this one from Terling in Essex, make sad entries in the parish registers:

> Buried 9 December 1592
> A poor woman who died in the barne at the parsonage whose name we could not learne.

Reflect

What can this source tell us about attitudes towards vagrants in the late sixteenth century?

What mattered to the Elizabethans?

The causes of the crisis

The fundamental reason for the increase in poverty after 1580 was the growth in population. The number of people in England had been growing from 1520 when the population was around 2.4 million. By 1600, the population had risen to 4.1 million. In order to feed this growing population more land was brought into cultivation and new farming methods were introduced, but English agriculture failed to fully meet the increased demand for food. The clearest indication of this was the steady rise in prices during this period. During the later sixteenth century, the price of all goods rose, but food prices increased more than anything else. In particular, as you can see from the graph opposite, the price of wheat soared. Yeoman farmers enjoyed increased income, but the wages of poor labourers failed to keep up with the rising price of bread.

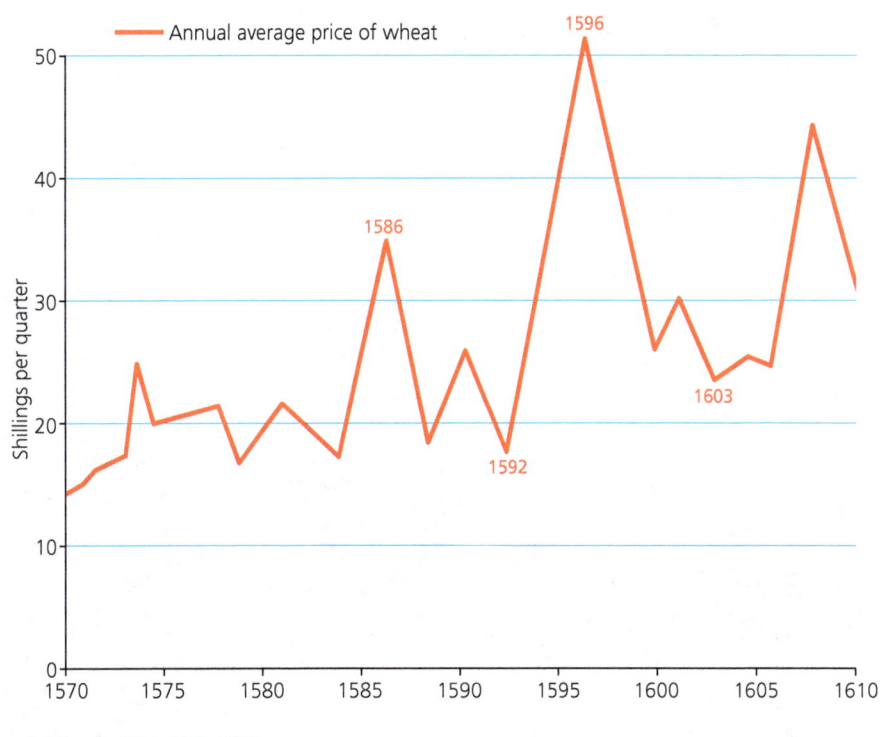

▲ Wheat prices, 1570–1610

The increase in population and prices caused serious difficulties for the labouring poor. In the 1580s and 1590s these long-term problems were made worse by three short-term pressures:

1. In 1586, and then again in 1595, 1596 and 1597, the harvests failed because of bad weather. Food prices rocketed.
2. From the early 1580s, there was a downturn in demand for English woollen cloth which further increased unemployment and the numbers of vagrants looking for work.
3. More frequent outbreaks of plague caused disruption to local economies and added to people's misery.

These changes placed late Elizabethan society under severe pressure. For poor families it was a time of crisis. Between 1597 and 1599, large areas of England suffered from famine. Historians have traced death from starvation through the huge increases in burials in parish registers across Cumbria, Yorkshire, Northumberland, Staffordshire and Devon.

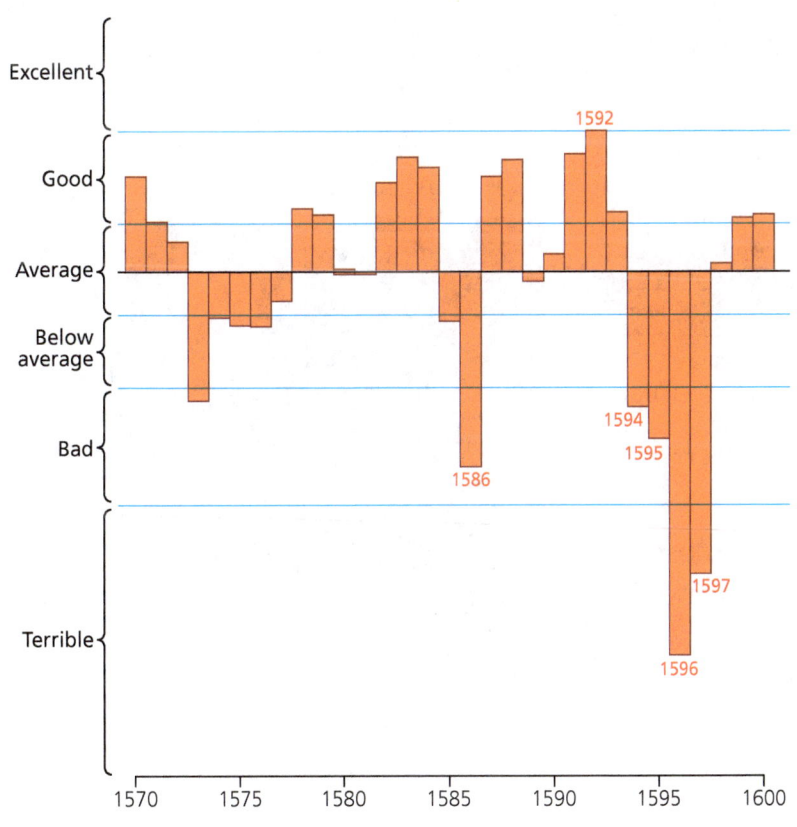

▲ Harvests, 1570–1600

Responding to the problem

The late Elizabethans divided the unemployed poor into three categories:

1. the **impotent poor** who were physically unable to work through age or illness
2. the **able-bodied poor** who wanted work but could not find it
3. **vagabonds** who chose to avoid work.

The government ensured that vagabonds were harshly punished. From 1572 the law stated that vagabonds above the age of fourteen should be whipped and burned through the ear with a hot iron – the hole was to be as big as a penny. Anyone above the age of eighteen who became a vagrant having already been caught before could be hanged. In 1589, the government further tightened the law on vagrancy by prohibiting people from giving shelter in their homes to vagrants. People could be fined for sheltering vagrants.

The government was slower to make provision for the impotent and the able-bodied poor. It was often individual towns which took the lead in raising money to support the impotent poor and in providing work for unemployed people.

◀ Vagrants being whipped and hanged, a woodcut from Holinshead's *Chronicle*, 1577

York: a case study

Like many English towns in late Elizabethan England, York was under severe pressure due to a growing population of poor people. In 1588, the authorities in York took bold action to deal with the problem:

- The wealth of York's gentry and middling sort was assessed. They were forced to pay a 'poor-rate' which was used to help the poor.
- 'Viewers' were appointed to make lists of all the poor people in the city, and to place them in different categories according to need.
- People who were 'aged, lame, impotent and past their work' were given at least three halfpence a day so that they would not have to beg on the streets.
- People who could work were provided with wool and hemp and paid a small wage to spin in their homes.
- 'Rogues, vagabonds, strange beggars (people from outside the city) and such as will not work' were either put to work in houses of correction or banished from the city.

In the 1580s, many English towns introduced similar schemes for dealing with the problem of poverty.

▼ John Speed's map of York, 1611

What mattered to the Elizabethans?

The Elizabethan Poor Law, 1601

By the late 1590s, the problem of poverty in England was so great that the government was forced to take action. Beginning in 1597, the Elizabethan government introduced a series of Acts which tackled the problem of poverty. These Acts, which were brought together in the Poor Law of 1601, made provision for the impotent and unemployed poor as well as punishing vagabonds. The Elizabethan Poor Law of 1601 had three essential features:

1. In each parish the Justices of the Peace appointed four overseers of the poor who, together with the churchwardens, were responsible for the poor of the parish. These men collected a poor rate from all the house-holders in the parish, and the money was used to support the poor.
2. Begging was forbidden, and vagrants were whipped and sent back to the parish where they were born.
3. The impotent poor were looked after in almshouses and work was provided for the able-bodied poor. Anybody who refused to work was placed in gaol or a house of correction where they were forced to do hard labour.

◀ Greenway's almshouses, Tiverton. A photograph from 1896.

Some historians have criticised the Elizabethan Poor Law for its harsh treatment of vagrants, but others think that it was an important and humane advance in the treatment of impotent poor and unemployed people. The Elizabethan Poor Law did not solve the problem of poverty, but it did ensure that large numbers of people would no longer die if the harvests failed. From 1601, it was firmly established in England that looking after the poor was the responsibility of the state, and that it should be paid for through local taxation. This system of poor relief lasted until 1834.

Record

Write a clear and organised summary of the ways in which the Elizabethans tackled the problem of poverty.

Review

The historian Keith Wrightson has described late Elizabethan England as a 'period of crisis' for many people. How far do you agree with this view?

CLOSER LOOK 3

Inside Montacute House

Reflect

1. Read the labels and find out about some of the rooms in Montacute House.
2. How did the interior of the house reflect the wealth and status of an Elizabethan gentleman like Sir Edward Phelips?

On pages 46–47 you found out about Sir Edward Phelips and the Elizabethan gentry. This closer look takes you inside Edward Phelips' home, Montacute House, and helps you to discover more about the daily lives of the Elizabethan gentry.

▼ Montacute House, Somerset

The Long Gallery

This room stretched across the entire third floor of the house. On days when it was too wet to go outside, this was where the Elizabethan gentry walked and enjoyed the views of the formal knot gardens which surrounded the house.

The service rooms

This side of the house contained the kitchen, pantry, buttery and other service rooms where around twenty servants stored and prepared food for the Phelips family and their guests.

Inside Montacute House

The Best Chamber
This was where Edward Phelips and his wife Elizabeth slept in their beautifully carved four-poster bed. Feather mattresses and pillows, with sheets and pillowcases of fine linen made their bed very comfortable.

The Withdrawing Room
Sir Edward Phelips and some of his special guests would sit and chat here after dining in the Great Chamber. They might also enjoy a game of cards.

The Great Chamber
This was the most impressive room in the house. The stained-glass windows included the coats of arms of many local families. The Phelips and their guests enjoyed huge feasts here. After the meal, the tables were cleared away and guests were entertained with music, dancing, plays and masques.

The Great Hall
An impressive entrance room where visitors waited to see the Phelips family. In medieval times the Great Hall was where the whole household ate together, but wealthy Elizabethan families preferred to be more private and no longer dined in the Great Hall.

4 Merry England?

What lay behind changes in popular culture?

What lay behind changes in popular culture?

▼ 'A Fete at Bermondsey', by Marcus Gheeraerts the Elder, c.1570

Reflect

This superbly detailed picture was painted by a Flemish artist around 1570. It shows a village celebration at Bermondsey, now a busy part of London south of the River Thames.

1. Look carefully at the painting and find at least three interesting details.
2. Think of at least one good question which historians might want to ask about the celebration shown in the painting.

> **Reflect**
>
> Read the information below and decided how far you agree that the period 1580–1603 was a 'golden age' of culture.

A 'golden age' of culture?

We cannot be sure what people were celebrating in Elizabethan Bermondsey. Some art historians think that the painting may show a wedding feast, but it is hard to identify a bride and groom. Maybe it was a parish feast which some Elizabethan villages held each year to celebrate the saint's day of their parish church. Whatever these wealthy people of Bermondsey were celebrating, they certainly seem to have been enjoying themselves.

The painting gives the impression that life was good for the Elizabethans. It suggests that people wore fine clothes, had plenty of food and came together to feast, dance and enjoy each other's company. This 'Merry England' view of the period contributes to the interpretation of Elizabethan England as a 'golden age'. So too does the emphasis which some historians have placed on the cultural achievements of the Elizabethans.

Art

Some wonderful works of art were produced in England during the period 1580–1603, but, like the picture 'A Fete at Bermondsey', most of these were painted by foreign artists. The Queen and her courtiers might pay for portraits of themselves, but generally showed little interest in painting. Most English artists were mediocre painters, but one genius did emerge – Nicholas Hilliard. As a young man, Hilliard spent some time in the French court where he learned new artistic techniques. His miniatures are exquisite works of art.

▲ 'Young Man Among Roses', a miniature painting by Nicholas Hilliard, late sixteenth century

Music

This instrument, known as an orpharian, may have been given as a gift by Queen Elizabeth to one of her courtiers. Music was important to the Queen and to many Elizabethans. Thomas Tallis and William Byrd, composed beautiful church music for the Queen's chapel. From the 1580s, there were also important developments in secular music. Madrigals became popular and the musician John Dowland wrote some wonderful 'ayres' – songs accompanied by a lute. Tallis, Byrd and Dowland took English music to new heights.

▼ An orpharian reputedly made for Elizabeth I by John Rose, 1580

Literature

In the period after 1580, the growth of education, the spread of the printing press and the emergence of some talented writers led to remarkable developments in English literature. Poets such as Philip Sidney and Edmund Spenser transformed English poetry. Prose writers such as Richard Hakluyt and William Camden produced fascinating travel books and biographies. But it was the dramatists, especially William Shakespeare, who contributed most to the flowering of culture in Elizabethan England. More than anything else, it was Shakespeare's plays which gave the period a golden glow.

▲ A portrait of William Shakespeare, early seventeenth century

What lay behind changes in popular culture?

Popular culture

Shakespeare's plays were not only enjoyed by the gentry, but also by many of the 'middling sort' and labouring people of Elizabethan London. In contrast, few ordinary people had any connection with the elite art, music and literature which flourished in England after 1580. Instead, ordinary Elizabethans shared a rich and varied popular culture which brought enjoyment and meaning to their lives.

In the 1970s, some historians began to ask interesting questions about Elizabethan popular culture. They tried to discover exactly what brought ordinary Elizabethans together in their communities, how the people enjoyed themselves and what beliefs they shared. What historians discovered was very different from the 'Merry England' interpretation of the late Elizabethan period. In many towns and villages, divisions between rich and poor were opening up, popular festivities were under attack and innocent women were accused of witchcraft. In London, some people even wanted to shut down the new theatres and stop people seeing Shakespeare's plays.

The Enquiry

Historians generally agree that there were big changes in popular culture during the late sixteenth and early seventeenth centuries, but they have different views about what caused these changes. Your challenge in this enquiry is to develop your own explanation of what lay behind the changes in popular culture.

The enquiry focuses on three specific issues:

1. The decline in popular festivities

At the beginning of Elizabeth's reign, people enjoyed a wide range of popular festivities. Holidays throughout the year were celebrated with drinking, dancing, plays and sports. By 1603 many popular festivities had disappeared from villages and towns across England. **Why did popular festivities decline?**

2. Concerns about witches

Magic and witchcraft were an important part of popular culture in Elizabethan England. Witchcraft had existed since the Middle Ages, but in the late sixteenth century there was a huge increase in the number of women accused of being witches. Many were hanged for causing death by witchcraft. **Why were so many people concerned about witches?**

3. Opposition to the theatres

During the 1580s and 1590s, a new form of entertainment took off in London. Several purpose-built theatres opened and large numbers of people flocked to see the new plays performed there. Other people wanted to close down the playhouses. **Why were people divided over London's new theatres?**

As you find out about each issue you should collect information on A3 sheets. In the middle of each sheet make a simple sketch of the relevant picture above and write the corresponding question. Around each picture and question describe the main features of this aspect of popular culture. Use a different colour to explain why the changes occurred.

Popular pastimes and festivities

Ordinary people in Elizabethan England enjoyed a wide range of festivities and recreations. Towns and villages often had their own particular customs and forms of merrymaking, but four aspects of popular culture were found nearly everywhere: parish feasts, calendar customs, sports and alehouses.

Reflect

Find three different ways in which the villagers in Breughel's painting were enjoying themselves at the village feast.

Parish feasts

Parish feasts, sometimes known as 'parish ales' were an important aspect of Elizabethan popular culture. These festivals, which celebrated the saint of the local parish church, often lasted for several days. Often there was a procession followed by eating, drinking and dancing in the churchyard. Sometimes people enjoyed plays performed by travelling players or were entertained by morris dancers and hobby-horses. People took part in rough sports and enjoyed recreations such as bull-baiting and cock-fighting. Villagers brewed large quantities of ale for the parish feast and they often drank too much. No English artist painted a parish feast, but this painting by a Flemish artist, Pieter Breughel, shows people enjoying themselves at one in sixteenth-century Flanders.

▼ 'A Village Festival', by Pieter Breughel the Younger, 1632

What lay behind changes in popular culture?

Calendar customs

Many ordinary Elizabethans looked forward to the customs and festivities linked to the religious and farming calendar. Seasonal festivities were times for merry-making, when people could enjoy themselves with their friends and neighbours.

- **Christmas** began twelve days of celebration with much eating, drinking, singing of carols and dancing. In some places 'mumming plays' were performed by people wearing masks and disguises. In the apple orchards of southern England 'wassailers' sang around the trees and fired guns to scare off evil spirits.
- **Shrove Tuesday** was a day of feasting before Lent began. It was a time when young men enjoyed games of 'shrove-tide football'.
- **Whitsun** was a popular time for parish ales. In the north of England villagers took part in 'rush-bearing', carting rushes to the parish church and spreading them on the church floor.
- **May Day** was a time of much merry-making and drunkenness. Maypoles were erected on village greens or in churchyards, and 'summer kings and queens' were chosen to rule over the May games. Young people gathered greenery in the woods and sometimes stayed out all night.
- **Midsummer's Eve** was widely celebrated. Bonfires were lit and much ale was drunk. In some villages there was a tradition that people sitting in the church porch throughout Midsummer's night would see apparitions of people who were going to die over the next twelve months.
- **Harvest Home** was celebrated at the end of the farming year in August. For Elizabethan villagers this was a time of much feasting, drinking and dancing ... if the harvest was good.

Sports

Elizabethan popular culture included a range of sports and pastimes enjoyed throughout the year. Contests of bare-knuckle boxing, wrestling and 'cudgelling' (fighting with sticks) were common. Football was the most popular sport, but Elizabethan football matches were very different from the game we know today. They were often played between large numbers of young men from different villages or parts of a town. There were no pitches; instead, players fought for possession of the ball which they kicked and carried across the countryside or through the streets. There were few rules and many injuries.

Some Elizabethan sports involved cruelty to animals that seems shocking to us nowadays. Bear-, bull- and badger-baiting were widespread in the late sixteenth century. The animals were tied up and attacked by dogs, with people betting on the outcome of the fight. On Shrove Tuesday 'throwing at cocks' was a popular sport. This involved tying a cockerel to a wooden stake with a piece of string and throwing sticks or stones at the bird to see who could win the contest by killing it.

The alehouse

The most common aspect of popular culture for the Elizabethan middling sort and labouring poor was going to the pub. The alehouse was at the centre of village life and the number of alehouses in towns was increasing after 1580. The alehouse was where people went for beer, good company and a sing-song with their neighbours. But for some people the alehouse was a place of drunkenness, gambling and prostitution.

The decline in popular pastimes and festivities

In the 1970s, when historians began to investigate Elizabethan popular culture, they discovered something surprising. In many villages and towns across England traditional festivities and pastimes came to an end during Elizabeth's reign. The decline of popular culture began in the 1560s and continued into the first part of the seventeenth century. Parish feasts ended in many areas, May games disappeared, plays and morris dancing stopped. The decline was patchy and some places held on to their traditional festivities, but the overall decline was definite.

What lay behind the decline in popular festivities?

Historians obviously wanted to discover who or what lay behind the decline in popular pastimes and festivities.

- **Was it the Queen?** No! Elizabeth appreciated traditional forms of festivity. Christmas was always enjoyed at court with music, dancing, plays, jesters and hobby-horses. The Queen was also fond of the May games and Midsummer celebrations. It was certainly not the monarch who lay behind the decline of calendar customs.
- **Was it the Privy Council?** No! Privy councillors were in favour of traditional festivities providing they did not become too unruly. In 1589, for example, the Privy Council supported people in Oxfordshire who wanted to keep up the tradition of maypoles.
- **Was it the Church?** Generally not. Historians found some cases of bishops banning traditional festivities such as morris dancing and maypoles, but these were rare. Most bishops did not attack calendar customs.

The Puritans

The people behind the decline in popular customs and festivities were the Puritan ministers who began to gain control of some parishes during Elizabeth's reign. The Puritans were extreme Protestants who wanted everyone to obey the bible and live pure, holy lives. During Elizabeth's reign, Puritan ministers began a campaign to improve people's behaviour. They preached sermons and wrote pamphlets, attacking many aspects of popular culture.

In some areas, Puritan ministers gained the support of the local gentry who were Justices of the Peace, and the middling sort who were village constables and churchwardens. It was particularly in the communities ruled by a Puritan elite that popular festivities came under attack. The following examples give an impression of what happened in different counties:

> **Reflect**
>
> What can the cases below tell us about the concerns of the Puritans?

Lancashire, 1587

The Puritan preacher, Edward Fleetwood persuaded the local gentry to ban all music, dancing and drinking on Sundays.

Hertfordshire, 1589

William Dyke, a Puritan minister tried to ban one of the church ales which had survived. The ale included a Robin Hood play and Dyke objected to Maid Marian (played by a man) coming into the church, kissing people and making them laugh.

Oxfordshire, 1589

A Puritan minister and his uncle, who was a high constable, issued an order banning all maypoles, church ales, May games and morris dancers in the villages around Banbury.

Devon, 1595

Parish ales had already been banned on Sundays. Now the Justices of the Peace abolished Sunday plays and May games. Ales could only take place in daylight and without music or dancing. Drink had to be provided by a licensed alehouse keeper.

What lay behind changes in popular culture?

The concerns of the Puritans

A popular interpretation of Puritans is that they were killjoys who simply wanted to stop people having fun. Historians, however, have tried to develop a deeper understanding of what drove the Puritans to attack popular festivities. They suggest that the Puritan ministers had five main concerns:

1. **Protecting the Sabbath**. Puritans thought that Sundays should be for rest and prayer. They were particularly keen to stop people dancing, drinking in the alehouse and merry-making on the Lord's day.
2. **Stopping Catholic practices**. Puritans objected to some popular customs because they were associated with the Catholic Church which had existed in England before the Protestant Reformation.
3. **Stopping pagan practices**. Some popular festivities such as Christmas candles, feasting, mumming, maypoles and Midsummer bonfires could be traced back to pagan times. The Puritans felt they were inappropriate in Christian communities.
4. **Preventing disorder**. Sometimes unruly crowds at popular festivities became violent and disorderly. The Puritans were concerned about this as they were trying to create orderly, 'godly communities'.
5. **Preventing unwanted pregnancies**. Puritan ministers complained that dancing and drunkenness could lead people to the sin of sex outside marriage. The May games, in particular, were a traditional time for love-making and were therefore a particular focus of complaint from ministers.

> **Record**
> Create your first A3 sheet to describe the main features of popular pastimes and festivities, and explain why these declined.

▼ Morris dancers by the River Thames, c.1620. In many areas, morris dancing came to an end in the later years of Elizabeth's reign

The persecution of witches

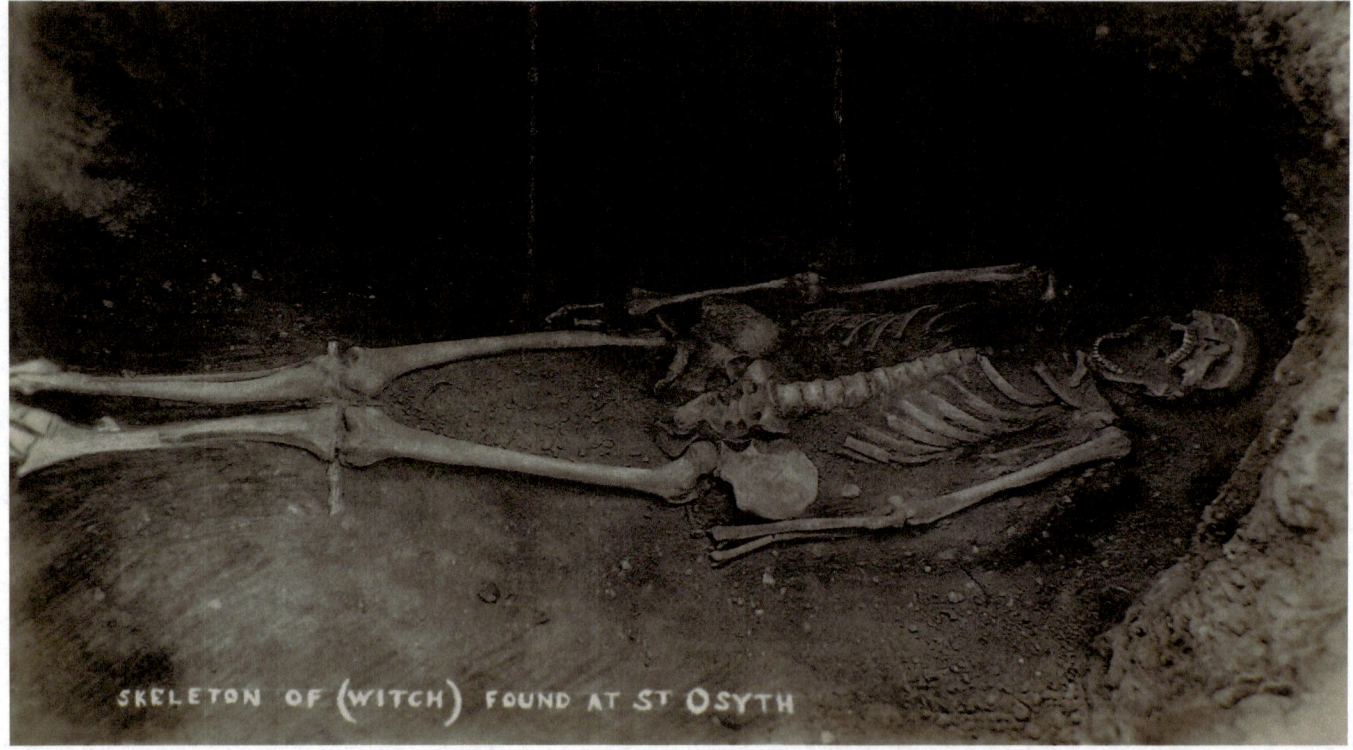

▲ A photograph of a skeleton believed to be that of Ursula Kemp, c.1921

In 1921, Charles Brooker was doing some building work at his house in the Essex village of St Osyth and was shocked to uncover a skeleton in his garden. Charles was interested in local history and knew that it was unusual for skeletons to be found outside a church burial ground. He believed that the skeleton belonged to Ursula Kemp, a St Osyth woman executed for witchcraft in 1582. When Charles Brooker examined the skeleton he was surprised to find that iron rivets had been hammered into Ursula Kemp's knees and elbows. Elizabethans believed that this was a way of stopping witches rising from the grave.

> ## Reflect
> Can you see any evidence in the photograph of the rivets in Ursula Kemp's elbows and knees?

During the early 1920s, many people were fascinated by witchcraft and Charles Brooker decided to make money from his discovery by charging people to see the skeleton. The photograph of Ursula Kemp's skeleton above appeared on a postcard from the time. In the 1960s, the skeleton was sold to the witchcraft museum at Boscastle in Cornwall and was later owned by an eccentric Cornish artist. In 2015, Ursula Kemp was returned to St Osyth and was finally laid to rest in a plot provided by the parish council.

Ursula Kemp was an Elizabethan 'cunning woman' – a healer and midwife. People in St Osyth and surrounding villages often asked her to cure their ailments and illnesses. When the young son of Ursula Kemp's friend, Grace Thurlow, fell ill, Ursula used a spell to cure him. Later, the two women fell out because Grace did not ask Ursula to help when her baby daughter, Joan, became ill. When she was a few months old, Joan fell from her cradle and died of a broken neck. There were rumours that Ursula Kemp had bewitched the child. Grace Thurlow ignored the rumours and again asked Ursula for help when she became lame. Grace Thurlow got better, but refused to pay Ursula Kemp her fee, saying that she could not afford it. The two women argued and Ursula threatened to get even with Grace.

In 1582, when Grace Thurlow's lameness returned and her son also became ill, she made an official complaint against Ursula Kemp to the local JP. She blamed Ursula for her own lameness, the illness of her son and the death of her daughter. In the trial which followed, Ursula Kemp's illegitimate eight-year-old son, Thomas Rabbet, testified about his mother's activity as a witch. Ursula Kemp was found guilty of causing death by witchcraft and was hanged.

Beliefs in magic and witchcraft

Ursula Kemp was one of many women accused of witchcraft in Elizabethan England. Historians have discovered a huge increase in the number of witchcraft accusations in the late sixteenth and early seventeenth centuries. To explain why this happened we need to understand the importance of magic and witchcraft in the minds of the Elizabethans.

Magic was an important part of the culture of Elizabethan England. Most people shared a range of supernatural beliefs which helped them to cope with the challenges in their lives. They might use magic to find out the sex of an unborn child, to cure an illness or to recover stolen goods. Magic gave people a sense that they could overcome difficulties and protect themselves against the uncertainties of life at the time. Magic was not seen as an alternative religion. At the beginning of Elizabeth's reign it was tolerated by the Church.

Most Elizabethans believed in magic, but some people known as 'cunning folk' or 'wise women' were thought to have special magical power which they had inherited. Elizabethans would often use these people for medical reasons, drawing on a wise woman's specialist knowledge of herbs and relying on her use of spells to make the remedies more effective. Ursula Kemp, for example, was known to be particularly good at curing arthritis.

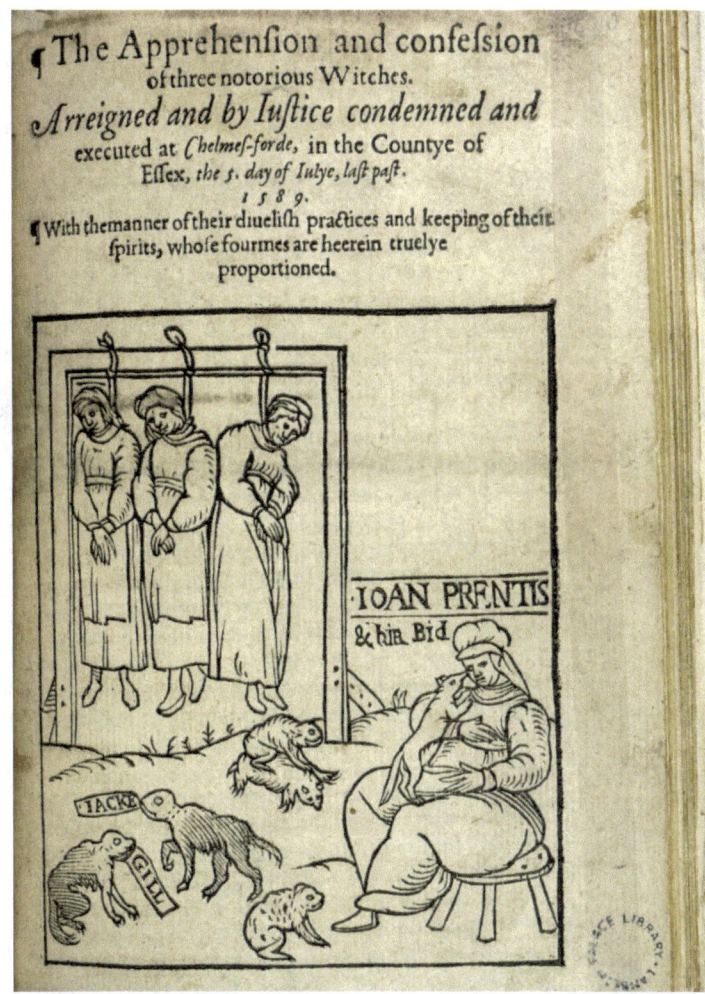

▲ The front page of a pamphlet describing a witchcraft trial in Chelmsford in Essex, 1589

> ## Reflect
> What can this front page from a pamphlet describing a witchcraft trial tell us about people's beliefs in witchcraft in sixteenth-century England?

Witchcraft, however, involved a special kind of magic which caused harm to people or their property. In Europe, witches were often accused of obtaining their power from the devil. It was thought that the witches met at sabbats where they feasted, danced and had sex with the devil. English witches were rarely accused of making a pact with the devil, but a popular belief in Elizabethan England was that they used small animals known as 'imps' or 'familiars' to commit evil acts. Ursula Kemp was alleged to have had four familiars: two cats, a toad called Pygin, and a lamb called Tyffin.

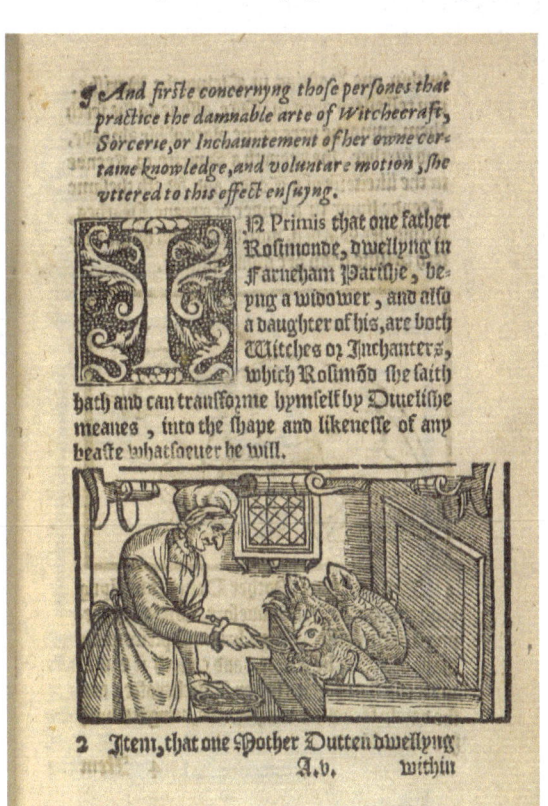

◀ An illustration of a witch and her familiars, from a pamphlet describing a witchcraft trial in 1579

▲ The number of witchcraft trials in south east England, 1560–1709

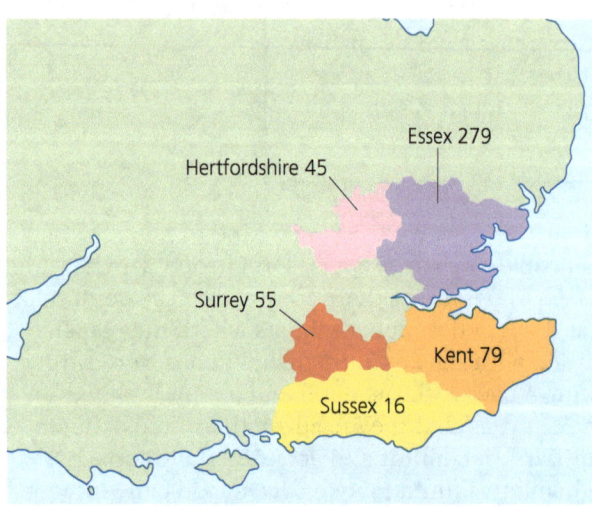

▲ The number of witchcraft trials in south east England, 1560–1701

Witchcraft trials

Prosecutions against witches in Elizabethan England were based on a law which was passed in 1563. This introduced death by hanging for a person found guilty of using witchcraft to kill someone. Witches who harmed people or property were imprisoned. It is difficult to get a clear picture of witchcraft trials because the legal records only survive for south east England and for the county of Cheshire. However, in the 1970s when historians began to examine the surviving records, they discovered three distinctive features of witchcraft trials:

1. Prosecutions for witchcraft rose dramatically in the late Elizabethan period

There were relatively few prosecutions in the years immediately after the 1563 law against witchcraft. However, the number of witchcraft trials shot up dramatically in the later years of Elizabeth's reign. There were 109 cases in the 1570s, 166 in the 1580s and 128 in the 1590s. These were the same decades which saw a huge rise in the population and big increases in poverty for many labouring people. In some years, poor harvests created tensions in many communities.

2. Prosecutions for witchcraft were particularly high in Essex

There were big differences in the level of witchcraft prosecutions in different counties. In particular, Essex, the county where Ursula Kemp lived, stands out as having a very high number of witchcraft trials. During the reign of Elizabeth, the heavily populated county of Hertfordshire just to the north of London had only 24 witchcraft trials. Sussex, a large county to the south of London, had only fourteen. In contrast, Elizabethan Essex had 172 witchcraft trials. Historians have been puzzled by the large number of cases in Essex.

3. Witchcraft prosecutions usually began with a complaint made by neighbours

In England there were few witch-hunts led by the Government or by the Church. Instead, prosecutions for witchcraft often started with complaints from neighbours. In a typical case a quarrel would occur between neighbours with one of them going away muttering and cursing. Then the other party would suffer a misfortune and would begin to suspect that they had been bewitched. They would talk to neighbours who might have similar suspicions and would then make a complaint to the local magistrate. It is possible that some of the accused women did practise magic and believed that they had the power to harm.

Historians' changing interpretations

As you know, historians often put forward different interpretations as to why things happened in history. Sometimes this is because historians use different sources, ask different questions or do not share the same values and attitudes. Often, however, it is simply because historians make their own judgements about the most likely causes. Over the past 50 years, different interpretations such as the ones below have been put forward to explain what lay behind the increase in witchcraft accusations in the later years of Elizabeth's reign.

Interpretation 1: Village tensions

When the historians Alan Macfarlane and Keith Thomas began their study of English witchcraft in the 1970s they suggested that the main reason for the increase in witchcraft accusations in the later sixteenth century was that these were years of hardship for many Elizabethans. People were less willing to give charity to their poorer neighbours. They were less likely to help a poor elderly woman who came to their house asking for a favour. If the woman cursed them as she left, and this was followed by some misfortune, they might accuse her of witchcraft. In this way, they transferred their guilt to the accused witch. For these historians, village tensions because of hardship lay behind the increase in accusations of witchcraft.

Interpretation 2: An attack on women

In the 1990s, some feminist historians saw the persecution of witches as an extreme form of the repression of women in the sixteenth and seventeenth centuries. They pointed out that the vast majority of people accused of witchcraft were women and argued that this was driven by the general misogyny of Elizabethan England. Not all feminist historians shared this view. Others pointed out, for example, that many of the people making accusations of witchcraft were women. It is certainly true, however, that the magistrate and jurors who judged Elizabethan witchcraft cases were always men.

Interpretation 3: Puritan concerns

Some historians have argued that as Protestantism became more established in England during the later years of Elizabeth's reign, religious concerns about the devil lay behind the increase in witchcraft prosecutions. It was in counties like Essex, where there were many Puritan ministers trying to establish 'godly communities', that witchcraft accusations were particularly high. Perhaps the drive against witches was part of the same process which brought an end to popular festivities and calendar customs.

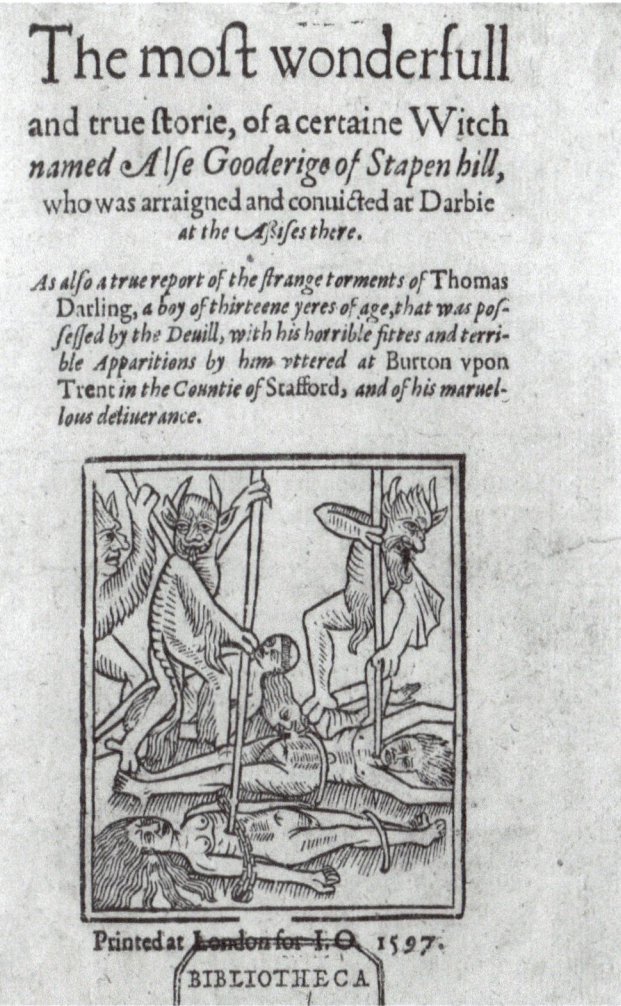

▲ The front page of a witchcraft pamphlet from 1597

Reflect

The picture from this 1597 witchcraft pamphlet shows the 'ungodly' being tortured in hell. These include witches and a Catholic friar. What can the pamphlet tell us about people's concerns about witches at the time?

Record

Create your second A3 sheet to describe the main features of Elizabethan witchcraft and to explain the increase in witchcraft trials.

Theatres and their opponents

In the last decades of the sixteenth century, a new form of entertainment transformed popular culture. The playhouses which were built in London after 1576 were England's first purpose-built theatres. One historian described the new theatres as 'an innovation in mass entertainment as radical as television in the 1960s'. People flocked to the new playhouses, but not everyone thought that they were a good thing. During the period 1580–1603, some people were fierce opponents of the theatres.

The new theatres

At the beginning of Elizabeth's reign, people had enjoyed miracle plays (sometimes called 'mystery plays') which reconstructed scenes from the Bible. These religious plays were sometimes sponsored by the craft guilds in different towns and were often performed on carts in the streets. During the 1560s and 1570s, Elizabeth's Privy Council had banned miracle plays as they saw them as a Catholic tradition.

Groups of actors still performed secular plays in marketplaces and inn-yards, but they faced an increasing threat of being arrested as vagabonds. In London, actors staged afternoon plays at inns, but the city authorities often tried to restrict them because they were too rowdy. Only the acting companies with a noble patron were secure. Companies like the Lord Admiral's Men or the Lord Chamberlain's Men performed in the houses of the nobility and at court. The Queen loved to watch plays and some of her leading courtiers sponsored a theatre company to win her favour.

Then, in 1576, Elizabethan theatre took a new direction. John Brayne and James Burbage paid for a new building in Shoreditch, outside the city walls, which would be used just for performing plays. It was the only one of its kind so they simply called it 'The Theatre'. The following year, a second theatre, The Curtain, opened nearby. In the 1580s and 1590s, more new theatres opened outside the city on the south bank of the River Thames. In 1587, the Rose Theatre opened near some existing bear-baiting and bull-baiting arenas. Eight years later, The Swan theatre opened nearby. In 1599, The Theatre at Shoreditch was taken down and was rebuilt in Bankside as The Globe. It was in this famous theatre that some of Shakespeare's greatest plays were first performed.

▼ The main Elizabethan theatres in London

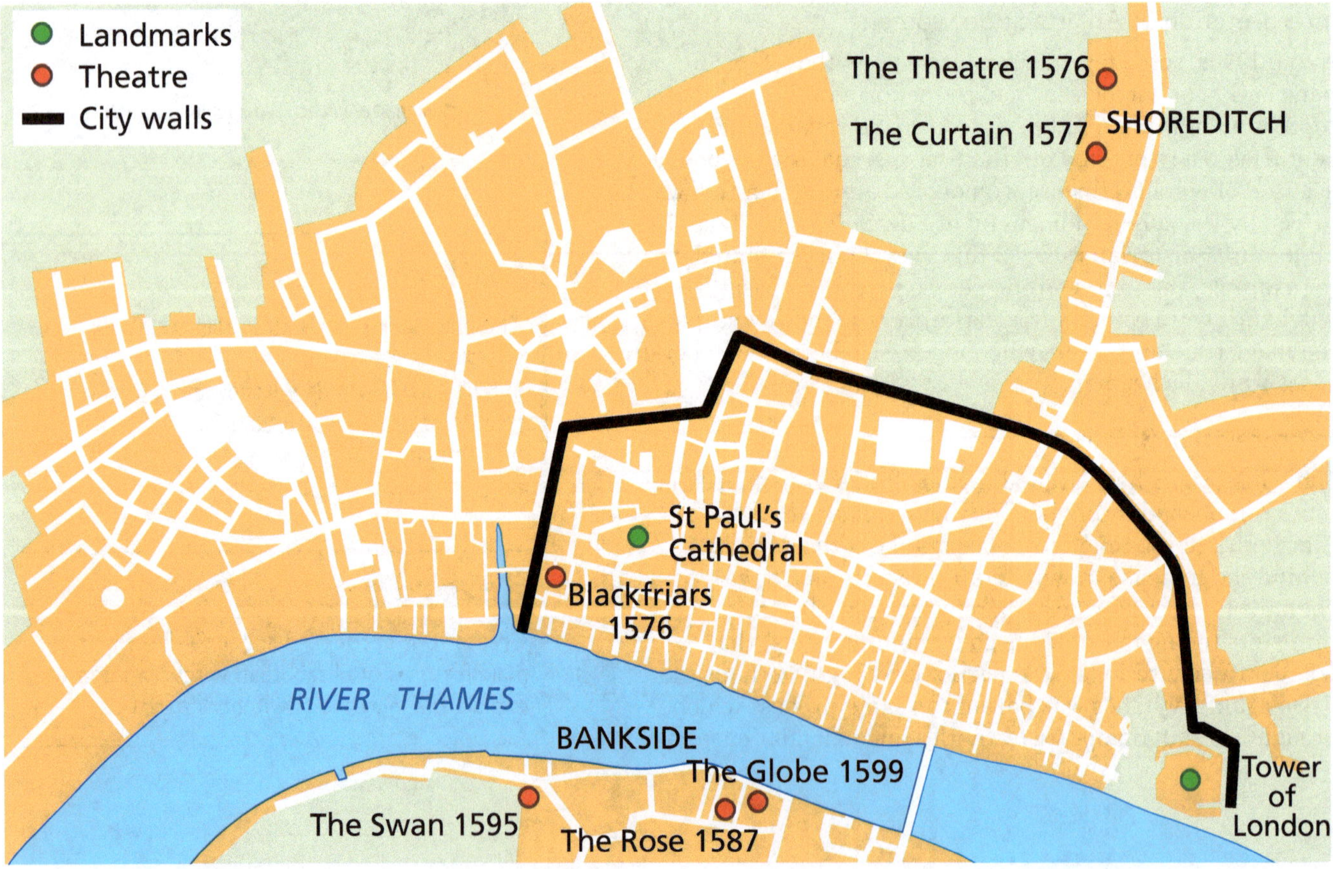

What lay behind changes in popular culture?

What the new theatres looked like

A Dutch traveller, Johannes de Witt, went to see a play at the Swan theatre in 1595, soon after it opened. He included this sketch of the interior of The Swan in a letter he wrote to a friend in the Netherlands. It is the only drawing of a theatre which survives from the Elizabethan period.

> ### Reflect
> 1. Find the following features in de Witt's drawing:
>   a) The **yard** (sometimes called the 'pit') was where poor people, known as 'groundlings' stood to watch the plays. They were very close to the actors.
>   b) The **stage** was raised about two metres from the ground and projected into the pit of the theatre.
>   c) The **galleries**. There were three galleries of covered seats around the pit. People paid extra to sit here.
>   d) The **roof** covered part of the stage, but most of the theatre was open to the sky. Plays were performed in the afternoon rather than the evening as there was no artificial lighting.
>   e) The **trumpeter** who announced that the play was about to begin.
> 2. In what ways were Elizabethan theatres different from most modern theatres?

Shakespeare's Globe theatre which opened on Bankside in 1599 lasted only fourteen years. In 1613, during a performance of Shakespeare's *Henry VIII*, a stage cannon set fire to the thatched roof. Within two hours the theatre had burned to the ground. It was quickly rebuilt with a tile roof and remained open until it was finally closed by England's Puritan administration in 1642. The building was demolished in 1644.

In 1997 a replica of the Globe theatre opened on Bankside. Johannes de Witt's drawing was a vital piece of evidence for the design of the new theatre.

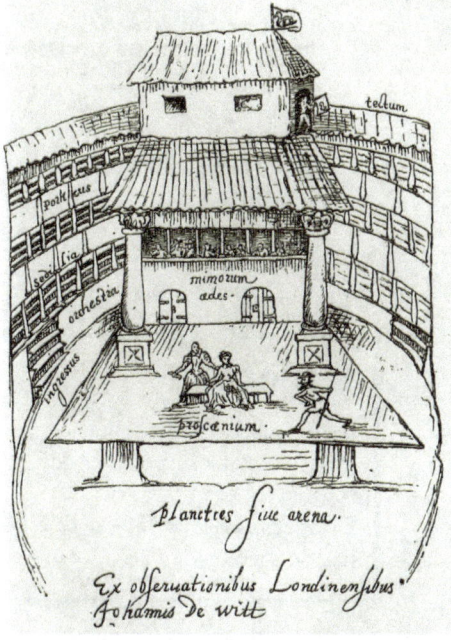

▲ A drawing of the Swan theatre by Johannes de Witt, 1595

> ### Reflect
> Which features from Johannes de Witt's drawing were included in the design of the new Globe theatre?

◀ Modern 'groundlings' enjoying a play at the new Globe theatre

The attractions of Bankside

From the 1580s, the afternoon plays at the new theatres on Bankside attracted thousands of Londoners and visitors. Elizabethans of all social groups loved the comedies, tragedies and histories written by Shakespeare and other playwrights of the time. The plays were full of strong characters portraying a range of human emotions. Never before had audiences seen so much energy, passion and drama on stage. If people stayed on after the play had ended they could enjoy the additional treat of a 'jig', featuring songs, dancing and jokes. Some Elizabethans complained that jigs were vulgar, but most theatre-goers enjoyed the rude and slapstick comedy.

The new theatres were bustling, rowdy places. Groundlings paid only a penny. An extra penny would buy a seat in one of the covered galleries. People moved around the yard selling nuts, fruit, shellfish and beer. Richer people in the galleries often took their own, more expensive, food. Cut-purses and pick-pockets mingled among the crowds. Fights sometimes broke out in the yard. Elizabethan audiences were noisy. People often called out to the actors and chatted through any dull bits. Eating, drinking, swearing, cheering and flirting were all part of an afternoon at the theatre for the Elizabethans.

Bankside had other attractions in addition to the new theatres. Many people took a small boat across the river during the morning and enjoyed a midday meal in one of Bankside's many inns. Before the play, they could watch a bear-baiting or bull-baiting in one of Bankside's two arenas for blood-sports. In the evening, many young men headed for Bankside's alehouses, bowling alleys and gambling dens. Casual sexual encounters were common and sex could always be bought at one of Bankside's licensed brothels or 'stews'.

▼ A recent painting of The Rose theatre and Bankside, by the artist Peter Jackson

> **Reflect**
>
> In the painting below, the artist Peter Jackson has tried to portray the reality of Elizabethan Bankside. How has he done this?

What lay behind changes in popular culture?

Opposition to the theatre

The London theatres divided Elizabethans. Some people saw them as a threat to society and argued that theatres should be closed. Opposition came from two main groups.

The London authorities

The new theatres were built deliberately beyond the city walls, outside the area controlled by London's mayor and alderman. However, the authorities were concerned that large theatre crowds created disorder in the suburbs of Bankside and Shoreditch. The mayor and aldermen also argued that the theatres drew servants and apprentices away from their work, and attracted the wrong sort of people including rogues, thieves and prostitutes. At times of plague, the large crowds of people at the theatres contributed to the spread of disease. The authorities wrote many letters to the Privy Council asking for the closure of theatres.

> **A letter from the Lord Mayor and aldermen of London to the Privy Council, July 1597**
>
> Theatres are places for vagrants, masterless-men, thieves, horse-stealers, whoremongers, cheats, swindlers, traitors and other idle and dangerous persons to meet together to the great displeasure of Almighty God and the hurt and annoyance of her Majesty's people. They maintain idleness in such persons as have no work, and draw apprentices and servants from their work, and all sorts of people from attending sermons and other religious services, causing great damage to the trade and religion of this realm.

Reflect
What does the letter reveal about the concerns of the London authorities?

Puritan preachers

At the end of the sixteenth century, Puritanism was strong in London and several Puritan preachers wrote pamphlets attacking the theatres. Theatre had originated in ancient times so the Puritans associated plays with paganism. Theatre was also a reminder of the miracle plays which had flourished in Catholic England. In addition, Puritan preachers were concerned that the theatres and other attractions of Bankside led young people into sinful behaviour, particularly sex outside marriage.

> **An extract from *The Anatomy of Abuses*, by the Puritan preacher, Philip Stubbs, 1583**
>
> Do they not maintain vulgarity foolishness and remind people of false religions? Do they not encourage prostitution and uncleanliness? They are plain devourers of maidenly virginity and chastity. For proof of this, look at the flocking to theatres daily and hourly, night and day, to see plays where (there are) such suggestive gestures, bawdy speeches, laughing, kissing, winking and glancing of eyes.

Reflect
What does the extract reveal about Stubbs' concerns?

Elizabeth's Privy Council generally ignored the protests of the authorities and the Puritans. The Queen and her councillors enjoyed watching plays at court, and protected London's new theatres. Only during the plagues of 1581–82, 1592–93 and 1603 did they order the playhouses to close.

Record
Create your third and final A3 sheet to describe the main changes in the theatre and to explain why London's new theatres divided Elizabethans.

Review
Use your three A3 sheets to write an essay explaining what lay behind the changes in popular culture, 1580–1603.

CLOSER LOOK 4

May Day and the myth of 'Merry England'

May Day and the myth of 'Merry England'

At the beginning of Elizabeth's reign, May Day was one of the most popular holidays in villages and towns across England, but the festival declined in the later sixteenth century. May Day had originated as a pre-Christian festival celebrating fertility and growth. By the middle of the sixteenth century, the celebrations included the gathering of greenery from the woods and the setting up of maypoles on village greens and in churchyards. The maypoles were painted in different colours and were covered in flowers and herbs. A young couple were chosen as the 'May king and queen' and people enjoyed processions, plays, music and dancing around the maypole.

May Day was the target of hostility for Puritans who disliked the pagan nature of the festival. They also objected to the mixed-gender dancing and drunkenness associated with the festival. During the late sixteenth and early seventeenth centuries, maypoles in particular became a symbol of 'the battle for Merry England' in many communities.

In the nineteenth century, Victorian artists contributed to the 'myth of Merry England' through their nostalgic paintings looking back at the 'golden age' of Elizabethan England. The engraving on the left shows a May Day celebration in an Elizabethan village.

In more recent times, re-enactors have enjoyed depicting life in sixteenth-century England. Each year, at Kentwell Hall in Suffolk, re-enactors bring to life scenes from Elizabethan times. The May Day event is the liveliest re-enactment of the year with over a hundred people in Elizabethan costume taking part in processions, plays and dancing around the maypole.

> **Reflect**
>
> In what ways does the Victorian engraving contribute to the 'myth of Merry England'?

> **Reflect**
>
> In what ways does this modern re-enactment contribute to the 'myth of Merry England'?

◀ Re-enactors re-create a May Day procession at Kentwell Hall, in Suffolk, 2008

◀ 'The Maypole of Merry England', a Victorian engraving of a May Day celebration in Elizabethan England, c.1860

5

Going global

What did the Elizabethan adventurers achieve?

In 1870, the artist John Everitt Millais painted this imagined scene from the childhood of the famous Elizabethan Sir Walter Raleigh. The painting shows the young Walter and his brother sitting by the beach near their home in Devon. The boys are listening in wonder as a sailor points out to sea and tells them a story of adventure in faraway lands.

Walter Raleigh became one of the most famous adventurers of the Elizabethan Age. For Millias, and other people living in Victorian Britain, Raleigh was a national hero. In the minds of many Victorians, the voyages of Raleigh and other Elizabethan navigators laid the foundations for the great overseas empire which Britain ruled in the late nineteenth century. Millais's painting suggests that this episode from Raleigh's boyhood was where the British Empire began.

> **Reflect**
>
> Why do you think many people in Victorian Britain admired Millais's painting?

▼ 'The Boyhood of Raleigh', a painting by John Everitt Millais, 1870

What did the Elizabethan adventurers achieve?

Walter Raleigh grew up to be a soldier, courtier, politician, writer, poet and navigator. In 1584, Elizabeth I granted Raleigh a royal charter authorising him to establish England's first colony in North America. The colony would be called 'Virginia' after the 'Virgin Queen'. Queen Elizabeth would not allow Raleigh to sail with his fleet across the Atlantic because she did not want to be without him for several months. Walter Raleigh did not take part in the voyage to Virginia in 1585. It is puzzling, then, that he appeared in the illustration on this 1922 trade card.

In the 1920s, Liebig's Extract of Meat Company (which later became OXO) gave away 'trade cards' with their tins of meat extract. Children collected the cards and swapped them with friends. This particular trade card formed part of a set based on famous seafarers and was produced for French children in 1922. It shows Raleigh landing on the shore of North America with the 1585 colonists. Clearly, the illustrator was not going to let historical facts get in the way of a good picture, especially if it might help to sell a few more cans of meat extract!

◀ A trade card issued by the Liebig Meat Extract Company in 1922

Reflect

1. How did the trade card reinforce the image of Raleigh as a national hero?
2. Do you think it matters if interpretations of history like the trade card present a false view of the past?

The Enquiry

A wide range of popular interpretations have portrayed Raleigh and other Elizabethan adventurers as bold explorers who served their Queen and country. They have depicted the adventurers as brave men who made dangerous journeys across the oceans, claiming territories for Queen Elizabeth I which would later grow into the British Empire. In 2012, A.N. Wilson, a newspaper columnist and writer of popular history, stated:

> It is no exaggeration to say that modern history began with the Elizabethans. British explorers went out to every corner of the known world to form the foundation of power and prosperity for future generations.

In this enquiry you will decide how far you agree with A.N. Wilson. Did the Elizabethan adventurers begin to transform world history as A.N. Wilson suggests? Where exactly *did* they go? What exactly *were* their motives and achievements? As you find out about individual Elizabethan adventurers make an information card for each one. On the front of the card include the adventurer's name and summarise his achievements. On the reverse of the card summarise his motives.

Imperial ambitions

Dr John Dee

The brain behind Elizabethan travel belonged to Dr John Dee. And what a brain! John Dee was one of cleverest men in Elizabethan England. His interests included mathematics, astronomy, astrology, medicine and navigation. Dee was a valued adviser to the Queen on all matters scientific and astrological.

On 22 November 1577, John Dee rode to Windsor to discuss a matter of great importance with Elizabeth I. For the first two decades of Elizabeth's reign, England had been a small and isolated nation with limited wealth and power. In contrast, Spain had built up a huge empire in Central and South America, while Portugal claimed territories in Brazil, Newfoundland and the East Indies (part of southeast Asia, including Indonesia and Malaysia). John Dee had a plan to change this balance of power. He argued that Englishmen should search for new northern routes to the rich markets of China and the East Indies. At Windsor, Dee presented his vision of a great empire, ruled by Elizabeth, stretching across the northern Atlantic. The Queen, he argued, should claim her right to rule over North America by establishing colonies there. Dee used a new term to describe his vision – 'British Empire'.

John Dee produced a map and books to justify the colonisation of North America. He argued that the Atlantic voyages of John and Sebastian Cabot after 1497 gave Elizabeth a claim on America. He even suggested that America had been 'discovered' by the medieval Welsh King, Madog. John Dee gave the Queen and English navigators a vision of an empire to rival that of Spain. He was also able to offer practical help to the Elizabethan adventurers. At the beginning of Elizabeth's reign, English sailors had little experience of ocean sailing. John Dee's huge knowledge of navigation gave these seafarers the skills they needed to find their way across unknown oceans in the years after 1577.

▲ A portrait of Dr John Dee, by an unknown artist, c.1594

▶ The front page of John Dee's book on navigation

Reflect

What details does the image include in order to glorify the idea of the colonisation of North America?

Record

Make your first information card for John Dee.

What did the Elizabethan adventurers achieve?

Francis Drake

On 26 September 1580, Francis Drake sailed his ship, the *Golden Hind*, into Plymouth harbour (see pages 6-7). When Drake set out from Plymouth nearly three years earlier, he had little idea that he would become the first Englishman, and only the second sailor, to sail around the world. Drake's achievement was remarkable.

Few details are known of Francis Drake's arrival in Plymouth at the end of his voyage, but illustrators have sometimes tried to imagine the scene. This picture appeared in the May 1978 edition of a magazine called *Look and Learn*.

Drake's voyage, 1577–80

Francis Drake was a daring Elizabethan adventurer. In the 1570s, Drake made several expeditions to the Caribbean where he plundered Spanish ships and attacked their colonies. In 1577, he began the voyage which would take him to the furthest parts of the Spanish Empire. The plan was to sail around South America, seeking opportunities for trade and plunder in Chile and Peru before returning to England via the same route. Drake's journey did not entirely work out as planned:

▲ An illustration of Francis Drake's arrival in Plymouth in September 1580. From the magazine *Look and Learn*, May 1978

November 1577 – Drake sailed from Plymouth with five ships and around 170 men. He began his voyage by plundering small Spanish and Portuguese ships off the coast of West Africa.

Spring and summer 1578 – Drake's fleet arrived in Brazil and sailed south, in August they entered the Strait of Magellan, at the tip of South America. Drake claimed several islands for the Queen, before sailing into the Pacific. No English sailor had been there before.

Winter 1578–79 – Drake travelled north along the coast of Chile and Peru. He raided several native settlements and attacked Spanish ships carrying gold and silver.

June 1579 – Drake landed on the coast of California. He claimed the territory for Queen Elizabeth, calling it 'New Albion'.

Summer 1579 – Drake feared that if he returned to England by the same route he would be attacked by Spanish ships. He therefore made the decision to sail west across the Pacific. In the Moluccas (Spice Islands) he traded linen cloth for cloves, ginger and pimento. He then made the long journey home via the Cape of Good Hope.

September 1580 – Drake returned to England. His ship was packed with vast quantities of pillaged treasure. Most of this was used to pay investors and to boost the Queen's treasury, but Drake was allowed to keep some for himself.

April 1581 – The Queen knighted Drake on board the *Golden Hind*. The King of Spain was furious as he thought of Drake as little more than a pirate. Drake saw himself as a good Protestant, a patriotic Englishman and a man who had earned his wealth through bravery and skill.

Reflect

How does the illustration above suggest that Sir Francis Drake was a national hero?

Record

Now make an information card for Francis Drake.

Elizabethan adventurers

In the years after 1580, inspired by Drake's voyage around the globe, Elizabethan adventurers attempted to take forward John Dee's vision of a 'British Empire'. Some adventurers focused on America, where they searched for gold and tried to set up England's first colonies. Others attempted to establish trade links with the rich markets of Asia (then often known as 'the East').

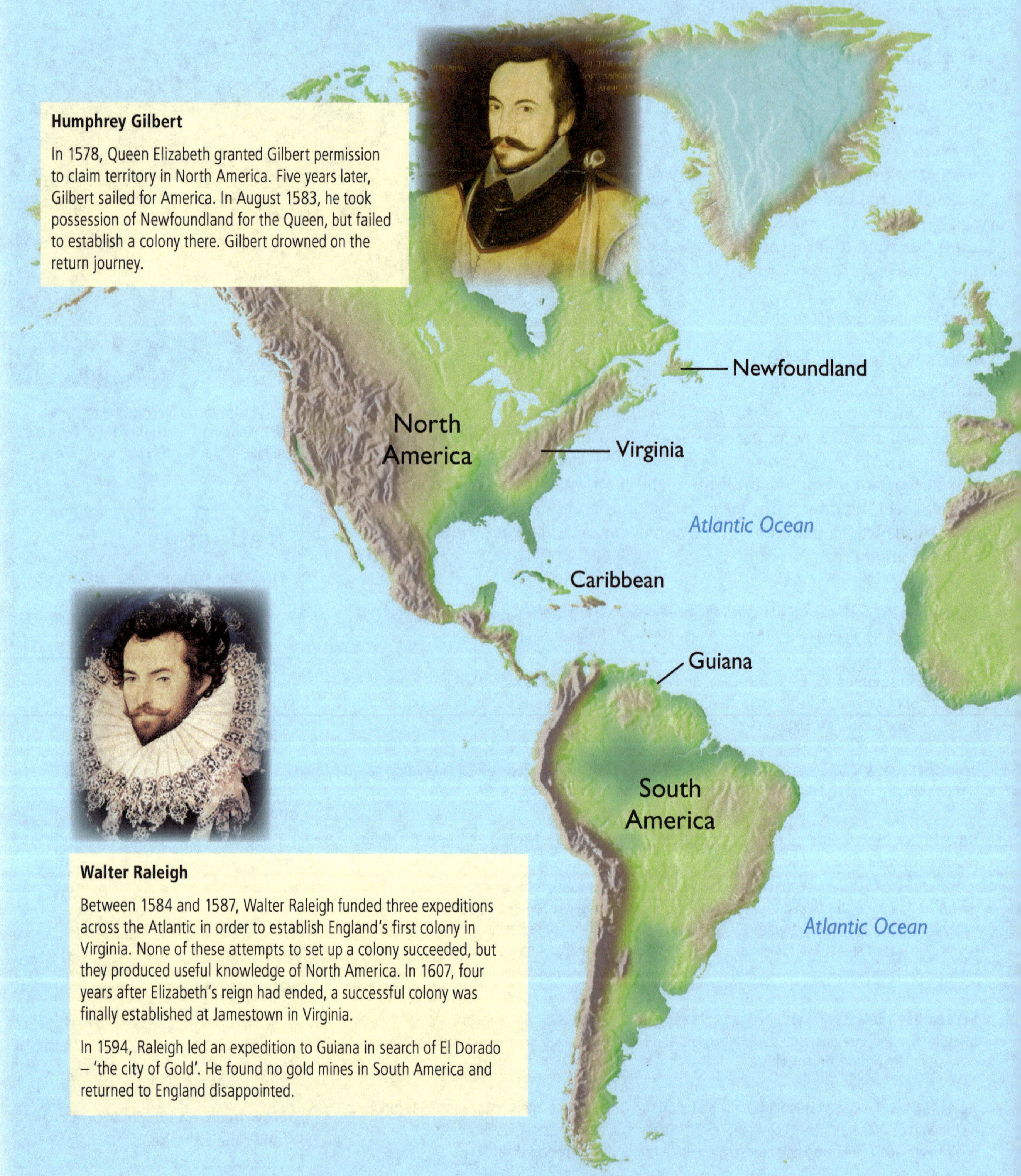

Humphrey Gilbert

In 1578, Queen Elizabeth granted Gilbert permission to claim territory in North America. Five years later, Gilbert sailed for America. In August 1583, he took possession of Newfoundland for the Queen, but failed to establish a colony there. Gilbert drowned on the return journey.

Walter Raleigh

Between 1584 and 1587, Walter Raleigh funded three expeditions across the Atlantic in order to establish England's first colony in Virginia. None of these attempts to set up a colony succeeded, but they produced useful knowledge of North America. In 1607, four years after Elizabeth's reign had ended, a successful colony was finally established at Jamestown in Virginia.

In 1594, Raleigh led an expedition to Guiana in search of El Dorado – 'the city of Gold'. He found no gold mines in South America and returned to England disappointed.

What did the Elizabethan adventurers achieve?

> ### Record
> These pages introduce the four adventurers whose stories you will discover in the rest of the enquiry. Use the introductions to begin an information card for each adventurer.

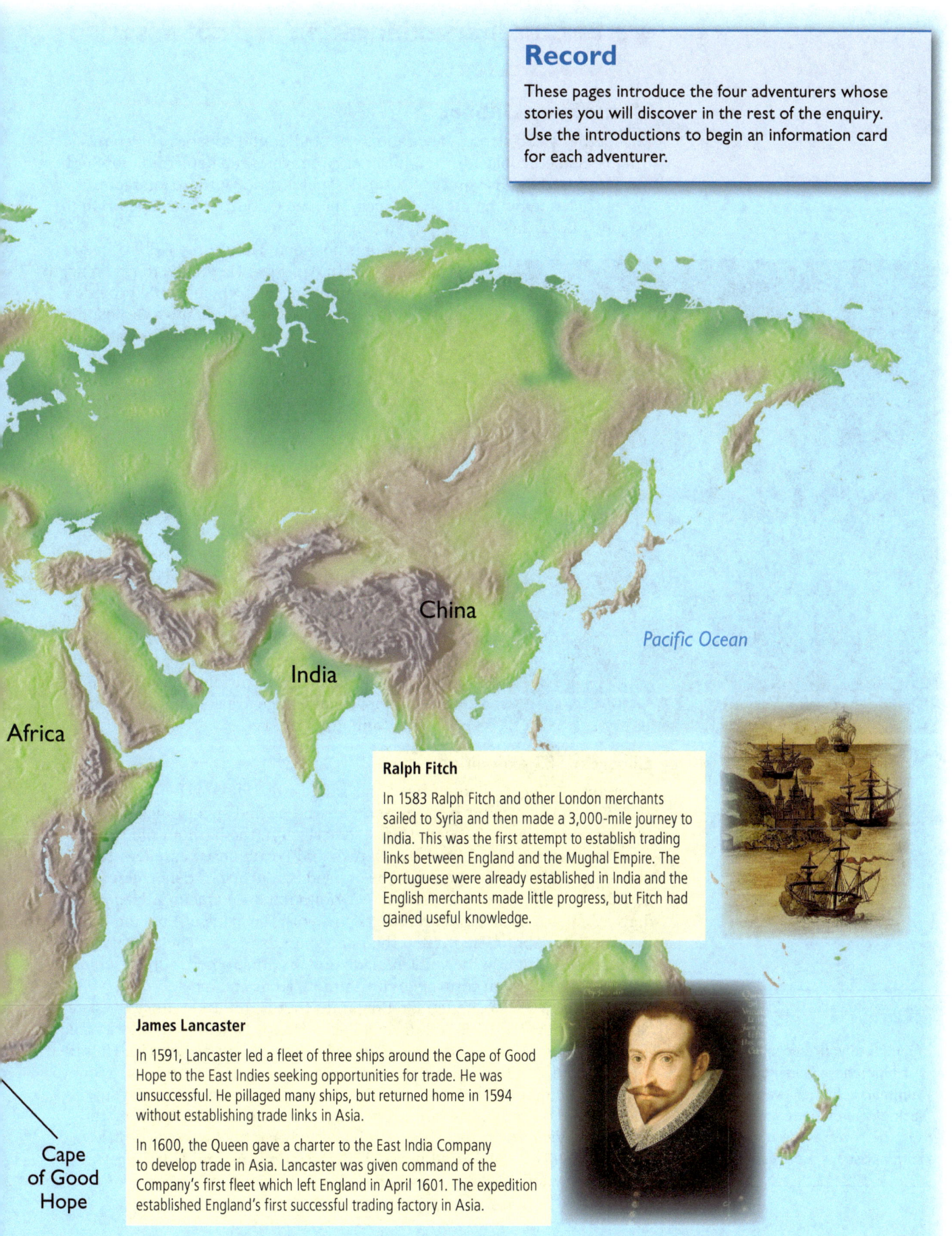

Ralph Fitch

In 1583 Ralph Fitch and other London merchants sailed to Syria and then made a 3,000-mile journey to India. This was the first attempt to establish trading links between England and the Mughal Empire. The Portuguese were already established in India and the English merchants made little progress, but Fitch had gained useful knowledge.

James Lancaster

In 1591, Lancaster led a fleet of three ships around the Cape of Good Hope to the East Indies seeking opportunities for trade. He was unsuccessful. He pillaged many ships, but returned home in 1594 without establishing trade links in Asia.

In 1600, the Queen gave a charter to the East India Company to develop trade in Asia. Lancaster was given command of the Company's first fleet which left England in April 1601. The expedition established England's first successful trading factory in Asia.

Elizabethan exploration and colonisation of America

Humphrey Gilbert

Elizabethans had strong views about the soldier and courtier Humphrey Gilbert. Some people admired his energy, bravery and determination. Others were repulsed by his vanity and ruthlessness. In 1583, these characteristics were witnessed by the men who accompanied Gilbert on his expedition to establish England's first colony in North America.

▲ A portrait of Humphrey Gilbert

Ever since his boyhood, Humphrey Gilbert had been fascinated by North America. He longed to find a north-west passage around America which would provide England with a trade route to China. As a Protestant Englishman, Gilbert was also driven by his hatred of Catholic Spain. In 1577 he had presented Queen Elizabeth I with his *Discourse How Her Majesty May Annoy the King of Spain*. It argued that a colony in North America would provide a base from which the English could attack Spanish ships.

In 1578, the Queen had granted Gilbert a charter for six years, giving him the right to establish a colony in North America. Gilbert's first attempt in 1579 was a disaster. Only the ship captained by his younger half-brother, Walter Raleigh, managed to cross the Atlantic. It pillaged several Spanish ships in the Caribbean and returned to England six months later in a sorry state. In 1583, Gilbert planned a new scheme. He would claim a vast territory in North America for Queen Elizabeth and sell millions of acres of American land to the wealthy Englishmen who invested in his voyage. Gilbert hoped that his ownership of a huge area of land in America would bring him great wealth.

Gilbert's 1583 expedition

Humphrey Gilbert's fleet of five ships sailed from Plymouth on 11 June 1583. Seven weeks later he glimpsed the land he had spent much of his life dreaming about. Gilbert's fleet had arrived in the harbour of St Johns, Newfoundland. Several English, Spanish and Portuguese vessels were already there as the harbour had been used by European fishermen for decades. Gilbert took possession of Newfoundland for Queen Elizabeth by digging a piece of turf and erecting a post with the arms of England engraved in lead. To celebrate, he invited the fisherman to a feast. The Spaniards and Portuguese brought wines, marmalade and biscuits. When Gilbert seemed ungrateful, they soon returned with salmon, trout and lobster.

Humphrey Gilbert had made England's first claim to territory in eastern North America, but he failed to establish a colony. Newfoundland was cold and barren, food was scarce and some of Gilbert's men became ill. He sailed his fleet south, but one of his ships was wrecked on Newfoundland's rocky coast and 80 men died. Those remaining were desperately short of supplies and insisted on returning home. On the journey across the Atlantic, the fleet faced violent storms. Gilbert refused to leave his overloaded little ship, the *Squirrel*. On 9 September 1583, the ship sank and Humphrey Gilbert drowned.

> **Record**
> Complete your information card for Humphrey Gilbert. Briefly summarise his achievement (or lack of it) in North America. On the reverse side of the card, summarise his motives.

What did the Elizabethan adventurers achieve?

Walter Raleigh

Walter Raleigh was determined to pursue his half-brother's dream of establishing a colony in America. Like other Elizabethan adventurers, he was driven by the possibility of finding a northern sea route from the Atlantic to the Pacific. Raleigh thought that America could be a gateway to the wealth of Asia. It also offered the potential to build an English empire to rival the empires of Spain and Portugal. Raleigh knew that it was the gold and silver mines of Central and South America which had brought enormous wealth to the Catholic powers. He hoped that gold could be found in North America, bringing him, and his country, great riches. In 1584, Raleigh must have been delighted when Queen Elizabeth I granted him a royal charter to travel around and colonise North America in return for one fifth of all the gold or silver that might be found there.

▲ A portrait of Walter Raleigh

The reconnaissance voyage, 1584

In April 1584, Raleigh sent his friends, Philip Amadas and Arthur Barlowe on two small vessels to explore the coast of North America. In early July they reached an island called Roanoke where they made contact with the local Algonquian people.

The reconnaissance voyage of 1584 convinced Raleigh that Roanoke would be a good place for an English colony. To persuade the Queen to invest in the colony, he asked his friend Richard Hakluyt to write a pamphlet explaining the benefits of colonisation. In his pamphlet, Hakluyt argued that colonisation would allow Englishmen to spread the word of God in America. He listed the many products which could be obtained in North America and suggested that it would provide a good market for English goods. Most important of all, a base in North America would allow the English to attack the Spanish treasure ships which financed Catholic aggression in Europe. Raleigh's propaganda worked and in 1585 he began preparations for the colony at Roanoke.

◀ A map of Virginia, 1586

Record

On the reverse side of your information card on Walter Raleigh, summarise his motives.

87

The voyage to Roanoke, 1585

Raleigh intended to lead the expedition to Virginia in 1585, but the Queen decided that she could not part with him for so long and he was not allowed to go. Instead, the expedition of 600 sailors, soldiers and colonists was led by Raleigh's cousin, Richard Grenville, and by the military commander, Ralph Lane. Also on board the fleet of seven ships which left Plymouth on 9 April 1585 were the scientist Thomas Hariot and the artist John White. In the months ahead, these men would produce a remarkable record of the landscape, plants, animals and people they encountered in North America. John White began by drawing one of the flying fish which sometimes landed on the deck of his ship during the voyage. Thomas Hariot produced the map which you can see on page 87.

The Roanoke expedition had a difficult journey across the Atlantic. Five days out from Plymouth the fleet was scattered by a storm off Portugal so Grenville's ship, the *Tiger*, sailed on alone. Grenville picked up supplies in the Caribbean and headed north towards Roanoke where he eventually rejoined other ships from the fleet. This stretch of the North American coastline was treacherous because of the long line of sandbanks which lay to the east of Roanoke Island. The ships got stuck on the sand at the worst possible time, just as a storm approached. The colonists lost most of their supplies including the seeds they had brought to plant. They knew that they would be dependent on the Algonquian people if they were to survive.

▲ John White's painting of a flying fish, c.1585

▲ John White's painting of a Native American chief, c.1585

What did the Elizabethan adventurers achieve?

Establishing the colony

At the end of July 1585, Ralph Lane took up his role as the colony's governor and began the urgent task of building a small wooden fort. This included houses, a storehouse, workshops and a church. The plan to settle 600 men on Roanoke was quickly abandoned. Instead, it was decided that Ralph Lane should remain with 107 of the colonists while Grenville returned to England for more supplies. Lane and his men began to explore the territory which the English had named Virginia, but during the autumn of 1585 lack of food became a troubling issue.

Wingina, the Algonquian Chief who ruled over Roanoke and neighbouring territory on the mainland, was wary of the English colonists. He knew that they would be forced to depend on his people for food during the coming winter months. At first, Wingina and his people supplied the colonists with corn, but the Algonquian began to run out of food for their families during the winter of 1585–86. Lane learned that Wingina was planning to attack the colony and he made a pre-emptive strike. Wingina was killed and the Algonquian became increasingly hostile. In June 1586, the colonists must have been very relieved when a fleet of ships, led by Francis Drake, came to rescue them.

Raleigh's plan to establish an English colony in North America ended in failure. However, the English adventurers had learned a lot about America. In 1588, Thomas Harriot and John White published a detailed account of this 'new world' in their *Brief and True Report of the New Found Land of Virginia*. The knowledge it contained enabled England's first successful colony to be established at Jamestown, Virginia, in 1607.

Raleigh's expedition to Guiana, 1595

In the early 1590s, Raleigh planned an expedition to the region of Guiana in South America. He dreamed of finding huge quantities of gold in the fabled city of Manoa, which the Spanish called 'El Dorado'.

Rayleigh's 1595 expedition did not find gold in Guiana, but in 1596, he published his *Discovery of the Large, Rich and Beautiful Empire of Guiana*. The marvels it described helped to ensure that English attempts at empire-building would continue into the seventeenth and eighteenth centuries.

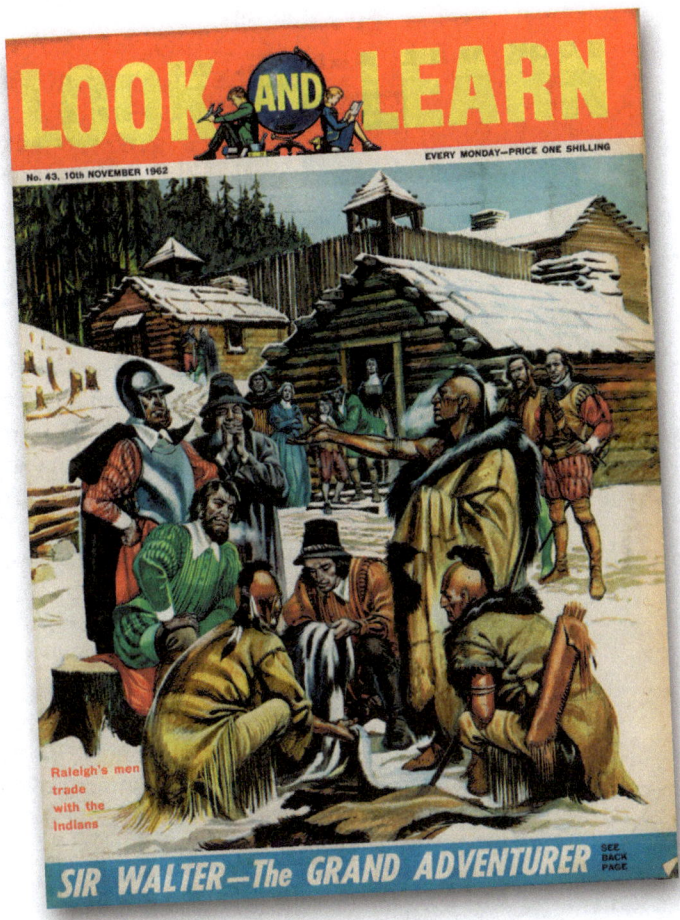

▲ An illustration of the colony at Roanoke in the winter of 1585–86. This appeared on the front page of the magazine *Look and Learn* in November 1962

> ### Reflect
> In what ways does this front page from the children's magazine *Look and Learn* emphasise Raleigh's achievement in North America?

> ### Record
> Add to your information card for Walter Raleigh. Briefly summarise his achievements (or lack of them).

Trade with Asia

In the 1580s, the increasing wealth of the Elizabethan gentry and middling sort led to a growing demand for luxury products from Asia. English merchants were keener than ever to import silk, cotton, jewels and perfumes from the markets of East Asia. In particular, they knew that huge profits could be made from the trade in spices. In an age before refrigeration, spices were crucial for preserving and flavouring food. Cinnamon, ginger, nutmeg, cloves, pepper and other spices could be sold for high prices on English markets.

Since the Middle Ages, spices had been brought to Europe along the overland routes which crossed Asia. Sea routes had also been developed by Arab traders who sailed from Arabia to the spice markets on the east coast of India. Eastern Mediterranean ports such as Constantinople, Alexandria and Venice became important hubs of the spice trade. At the beginning of the sixteenth century, the Portuguese were the first Europeans to bring spices from India to Europe by sailing around the southern tip of Africa. The Portuguese established forts and trading posts on India's east coast and were able to dominate the spice trade throughout the sixteenth century.

In 1580, when Spain invaded Portugal, English merchants feared that Europe's spice trade with India would be disrupted. To counteract this, they attempted to strengthen the trade links with Constantinople and the Ottoman Empire (modern-day Turkey), by forming the Turkey Company in 1581. The London merchants obtained a charter from the Queen which gave them a monopoly of trade in the Eastern Mediterranean. The merchants soon began to dream of developing direct trade links between England and India.

▼ Spices from Asia. Five of the most important have been picked out.

Cinnamon was obtained from the bark of a tree mostly grown in Ceylon (Sri Lanka). The Elizabethans mainly used it to flavour desserts.

Ginger was used in sweet dishes and drinks. The Elizabethans also used it as a medicine for digestive problems.

Nutmeg was grown in the Moluccas (Spice Islands). Ground or grated nutmeg was used to flavour a wide range of dishes in Elizabethan England.

Cloves were highly prized for flavouring meat and fruit dishes. They were also used as a fragrance and a cure for toothache.

Pepper was the most popular spice of wealthy Elizabethans. It was a luxury item used for flavouring foods.

What did the Elizabethan adventurers achieve?

Ralph Fitch's journey to Asia, 1583–91

In 1583, a London merchant called Ralph Fitch set off on a journey to India. He was accompanied by two other merchants, John Newberry and John Eldred, a jeweller called William Leedes and James Story, a painter. Of the five men who left England in 1583, only Ralph Fitch would return.

Ralph Fitch and the other adventurers had been commissioned by the Turkey Company to find out about the opportunities for trade in India, South East Asia and, if possible, China. They carried letters of introduction from Queen Elizabeth to the Mughal and Chinese emperors. In the 1580s the Mughal Empire and China were the greatest civilisations in the world. The adventurers hoped that the Queen's letters would persuade the emperors to begin trading with England. They also hoped that the Queen's letters would protect them on their long and difficult journey.

The adventurers left Falmouth on 11 March 1583 and sailed to the Eastern Mediterranean. They travelled overland from Aleppo in Syria and on to Baghdad, reaching Basra by May 1583. John Eldred stayed behind in Basra to trade. The others sailed down the Persian Gulf to the Portuguese trading station of Hormuz. There they were immediately arrested as spies and were imprisoned. Fitch and the other English adventurers were taken across the Indian Ocean to Goa, the main Portuguese colony in India. The men were eventually released, but James Story chose to remain in Goa, joining the Jesuit College. In April 1584, Fitch, Newberry and Leedes began their journey to the court of the Mughal Emperor Akbar, in northern India.

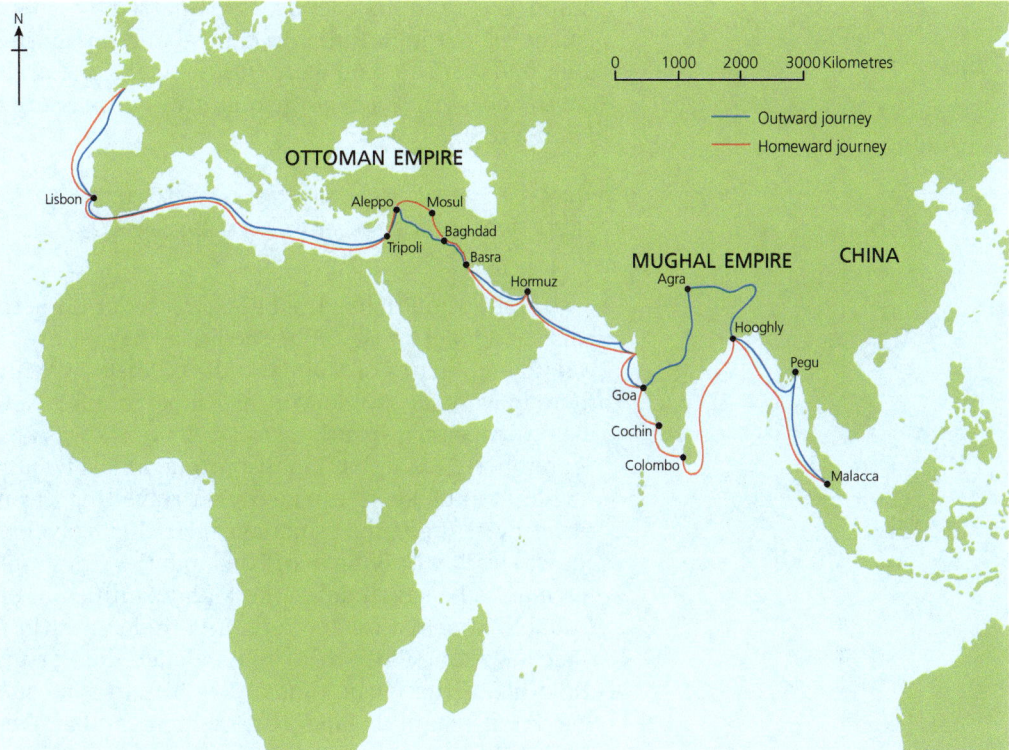

▲ A map of Ralph Fitch's journey, 1583–91

▼ Goa in the sixteenth century

91

To the court of the Mughal Emperor and beyond

Ralph Fitch and his friends were amazed by what they saw as they journeyed through India. In central and northern India they noticed large diamonds for sale and were impressed by the production of cotton cloth. On the coast they saw large quantities of peppers and other spices. Later, Fitch wrote:

> Here is much traffic for all sorts of spices and drugs, cloth of silk, elephants' teeth … and much sugar which is made of the nut called Gajara.

In 1585, the English travellers arrived at Emperor Akbar's newly built palace complex of Fatehpur Sikri near Agra. Here they saw the great wealth and luxury of Mughal India on display. William Leedes remained there to work as jeweller for the Emperor. John Newberry decided to begin his return journey overland to England. He was never heard of again. In September 1585, Ralph Fitch continued his adventure in Asia, alone.

Ralph Fitch spent the next year travelling through northern India reaching as far as the Himalayas. He then travelled to Hooghly, sailed across the Bay of Bengal and became the first Englishman to travel in Burma. As he sailed down the Malay Peninsula, Fitch picked up much valuable information about the sea trade with China and the Moluccas (Spice Islands). Early in 1588, he visited the Portuguese fort of Malacca but the officials there would not allow him to continue into the South China Sea. Fitch began his long journey home and arrived back in London on 29 April 1591. His journey had taken eight years.

Ralph Fitch was the first Englishman to find out about the possibilities of direct trade with South East Asia. For much of his journey he had travelled alone, relying only on his courage and the two letters from the Queen, neither of which turned out to be of any use. After his return, Fitch wrote an account of his journey which included descriptions of some of the people, customs and religions of Asia. People were fascinated by what he had seen, but what interested the London merchants most were Fitch's descriptions of the markets of India and of the gems, spices, cloths, drugs and dyes which could be traded.

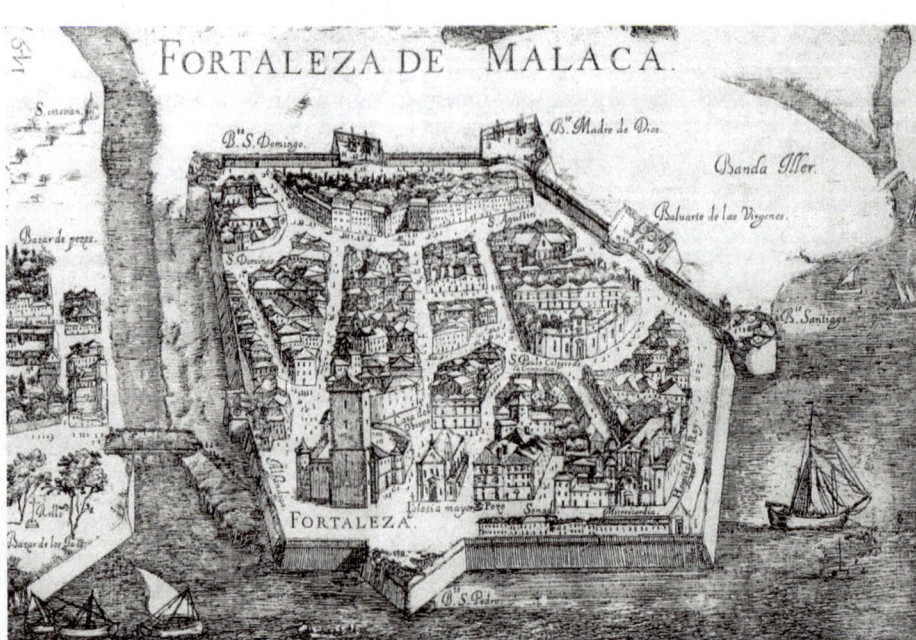

▶ Malacca, a detail from a seventeenth-century map

What did the Elizabethan adventurers achieve?

◀ Emperor Akbar inspecting the building work at Fatehpur Sikri, 1584. A Mughal miniature painting from the late sixteenth century

Reflect

What evidence of the wealth and luxury of Mughal India can you see in the painting?

Record

Make an information card for Ralph Fitch.

▶ A portrait of James Lancaster, 1596

James Lancaster

Just three weeks before Ralph Fitch returned to London in April 1591, the merchant James Lancaster sailed from Plymouth on a journey to Asia. In 1588, Lancaster had commanded the merchant ship *Edward Bonaventure* in the English fleet against the Armada. Now he was taking this same ship, with two others, on the first English trading voyage to the East Indies.

The voyage was a disaster. One of the ships sank on the outward journey. In the East Indies, the Portuguese prevented Lancaster from trading and he spent much of the time pillaging ships in the Indian Ocean. A terrible return journey meant that only 25 of Lancaster's men survived to reach England in May 1594.

Lancaster's first voyage to Asia was a failure, but he had learned a lot about the Portuguese presence in South East Asia. Six years later he would return to Asia. This time he would succeed.

Reflect

How does the artist suggest that James Lancaster was an important Elizabethan adventurer?

What did the Elizabethan adventurers achieve?

The first East India Company voyage, 1601–03

On 22 September 1600, over a hundred of London's leading merchants met at Founder's Hall to form a company that they hoped would transform England's trade in Asia – the East India Company. The merchants knew all too well that the attempts to establish a colony in North America had failed, that English adventurers had failed to arrive at a northern passage to Asia and that England had failed to establish a direct trade link with Asia around the Cape of Good Hope. In the summer of 1599, the merchants had been shocked to discover that a Dutch ship had returned to Amsterdam laden with 800 tons of pepper, 200 tons of cloves and huge quantities of nutmeg, cinnamon and other luxuries. The English merchants were desperate for the Dutch not to dominate Europe's trade with Asia.

James Lancaster was one of the merchants who invested in the East India Company. On 31 December, he was delighted when the Queen gave the Company a charter granting it a monopoly on trade with Asia. Lancaster was chosen to command the four ships which formed the East India Company's first expedition in 1601. He was also made the Queen's special envoy to various rulers in Asia. Lancaster's voyage of 1601–03 was a huge success. In 1602, he established England's first factory (warehouse) in Asia at Bantam on the island of Java. At last, English ships, too, began to return from Asia laden with spices.

When James Lancaster arrived back in England in September 1603, Queen Elizabeth I had been dead for six months. No overseas empire had been established in her reign, but Lancaster's voyage of 1601–03 was an important moment in world history. He and the other merchants of the East India Company did not know at the time, but Dr Dee's dream of a 'British Empire' had begun to come true. In the seventeenth century, the East India Company would open many factories on the coast of India. By the eighteenth century, it would rule vast areas of India and would become the biggest trading company the world had ever known.

◀ The East India Company trading post at Surat, established in 1613. Here goods from India were purchased and stored until a ship took them to England. Surat and other trading posts were set up following James Lancaster's voyage.

Review

As you know, one of the great things about studying history is that it teaches you to develop your own view on an issue, and to support your view with evidence.

You should now have six information cards which summarise the motives and achievements of **John Dee, Francis Drake, Humphrey Gilbert, Walter Raleigh, Ralph Fitch and James Lancaster**. Use these cards to develop your own view of the overall achievement of the Elizabethan adventurers.

The toughest questions in the GCSE exam will ask you how far you agree with someone else's view of a particular historical issue. You need to make a clear judgment and support your view with accurate details.

We began this enquiry with the following quotation from the writer A.N. Wilson:

> It is no exaggeration to say that modern history began with the Elizabethans. British explorers went out to every corner of the known world to form the foundation of power and prosperity for future generations.

Write an essay to explain how far you agree with this view.

CLOSER LOOK 5

Dead and *not* gone

At the end of January 1603, Queen Elizabeth left London to enjoy the peace and quiet of her palace at Richmond. In early March, she became unwell, losing her appetite and falling into a depression. The Queen refused any medicine and her physicians reported that she became increasingly confused. She refused to lie down, but her attendants finally got her into bed on 21 March. Elizabeth died three days later at the age of 70. She had reigned for 44 years and five months.

The Queen's corpse was embalmed and placed in a coffin before being taken on a black-draped barge from Richmond to Whitehall. For four weeks, her body lay in state on a black velvet bed in a chamber at her palace in Whitehall. On 28 April, it was taken to Westminster Abbey for burial.

The funeral procession

A thousand people formed the funeral procession and tens of thousands more filled the streets of London. One observer wrote 'there was such a general sighing, groaning and weeping as the like hath not been known or seen before in the memory of man'.

Shortly after the funeral, a long painting was made of the procession. The section below shows the most important part of the procession. On the left, four white horses draped in black, pull the chariot which carried the coffin to Westminster Abbey. On top of the coffin is an effigy of the Queen. It is surrounded by her most important courtiers, dressed in black and carrying the banners of the Queen's ancestors.

▼ The procession of Elizabeth I's coffin

Another section of the painting, which you can see on the opposite page, shows the Queen's Guard. On the left is Sir Walter Raleigh, Captain of the Queen's Guard. He wears a long black cloak and leads his ten guards, each carrying his halberd pointing downwards to signify mourning.

Dead and not gone

▲ The Queen's Guard in her funeral procession

The Elizabethan era had ended. In the seventeenth century, as England was torn apart by civil war, some people began to look back to the later years of Elizabeth's reign as a 'golden age'. In the nineteenth century, when Britain ruled the largest empire the world had ever known, many Victorians saw the seeds of Britain's greatness in the golden years of Elizabeth. In the early 1950s, at the start of the second Elizabethan era, some historians looked back to the first as a golden age of progress. Recent historians have developed more complex interpretations of the period, but the myths and realities of the Elizabethans continue to fascinate us in the twenty-first century.

▼ A conservator finishes off a deep clean of the tomb of Queen Elizabeth I in 2008, the 450th anniversary of the Queen's accession to the throne

Preparing for the examination

The British depth study forms the second half of Paper 1: British History. It is worth twenty per cent of your GCSE. To succeed in the examination you will need to think clearly about different aspects of The Elizabethans, 1580–1603 and support your ideas with accurate knowledge. This section suggests some revision strategies you might like to try and explains the types of examination questions that you can expect.

Summaries of the five key issues

Your study of The Elizabethans, 1580–1603, has covered five important issues from that time:

1. Elizabeth and government – the power of the Queen
2. Catholics – the nature and extent of the Catholic threat
3. Daily lives – the nature and dynamics of Elizabethan society
4. Popular culture – 'Merry England'?
5. The wider world – the nature and significance of England's connections with the wider world.

In the specification for your GCSE course, each of the five issues is divided into three sections. We divided each enquiry in this book into three stages to match these sections and to help you build your knowledge and understanding step by step.

Now you can use your knowledge and understanding to produce a detailed and accurate summary for each of the five issues. You will also need to be clear about how the five issues are connected. Here are four suggestions for structuring your revision notes and showing the connections between the issues. Choose the one that is best for you or use a variety if you prefer.

1. Mind maps

A mind map on A3 paper (or even larger) is a good way to summarise the important points about a particular issue. It allows you to show connections between different points. This is especially important in the British depth study as you are expected to show the interplay between issues (that is how one issue may affect others).

You could use colour-coding to identify a few really good examples of where in your mind map each of the following forces are at work:

- Political
- Religious
- Economic
- Social
- Cultural

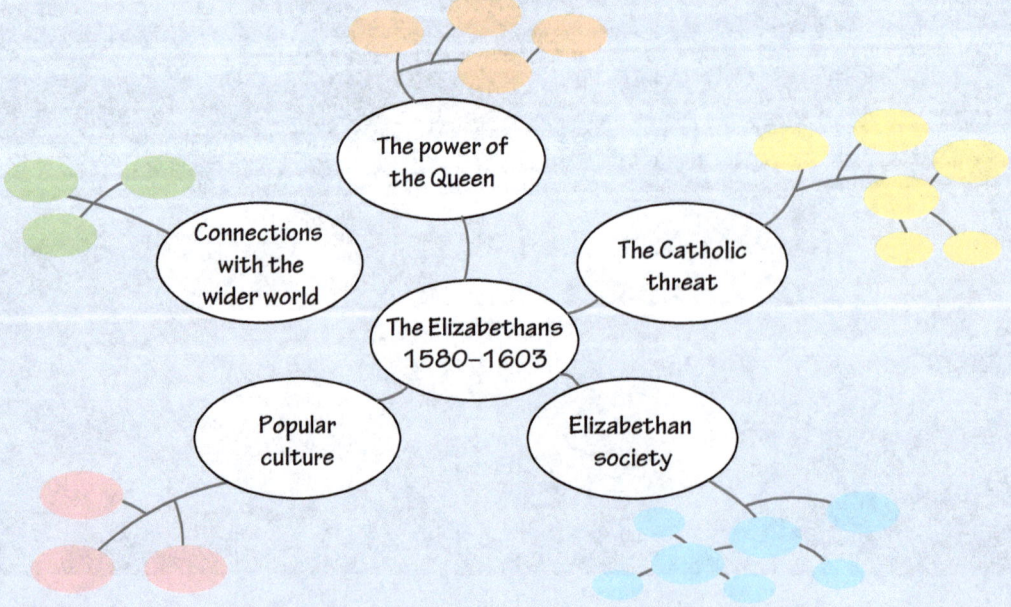

Preparing for the examination

2. Charts

If you find it easier to learn from lists then a summary chart for each issue you have studied might be best for you. You can use the format shown below or design your own. Just make sure that you include clear summary points for each of the three sections in each enquiry you studied.

To help you to remember how the five different forces are at work, you could use the colour-coding idea explained under 'Mind maps' on page 98.

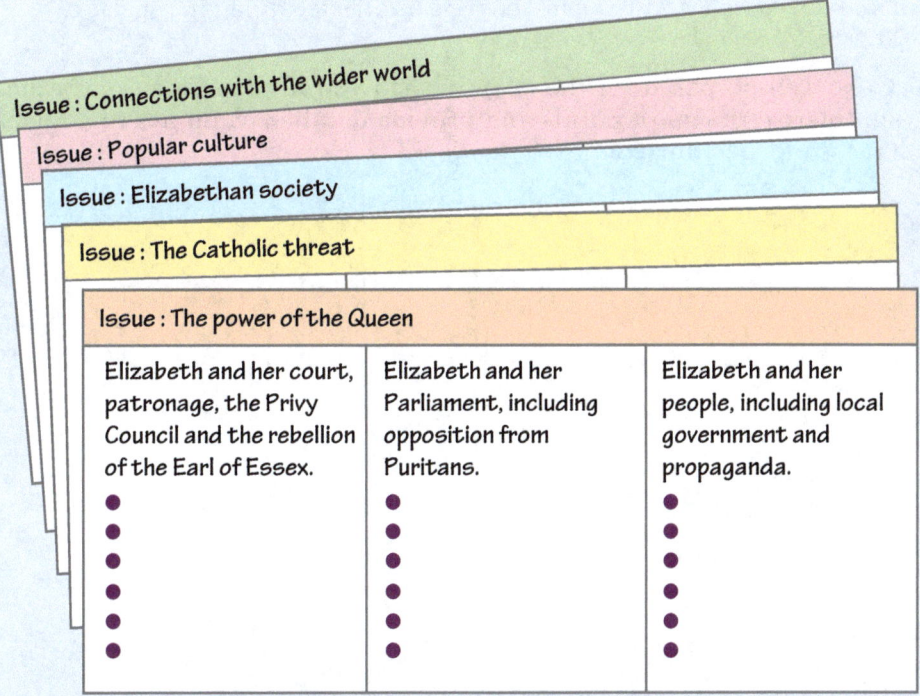

3. Small cards

Small cards are a flexible way to make revision notes. You could create a set of revision cards for each of the five main issues/enquiries you have studied. It would be a good idea to use a different colour for each set of cards.

To help you to remember how the five different forces are at work, you could use the colour-coding idea explained under 'Mind maps' on page 98.

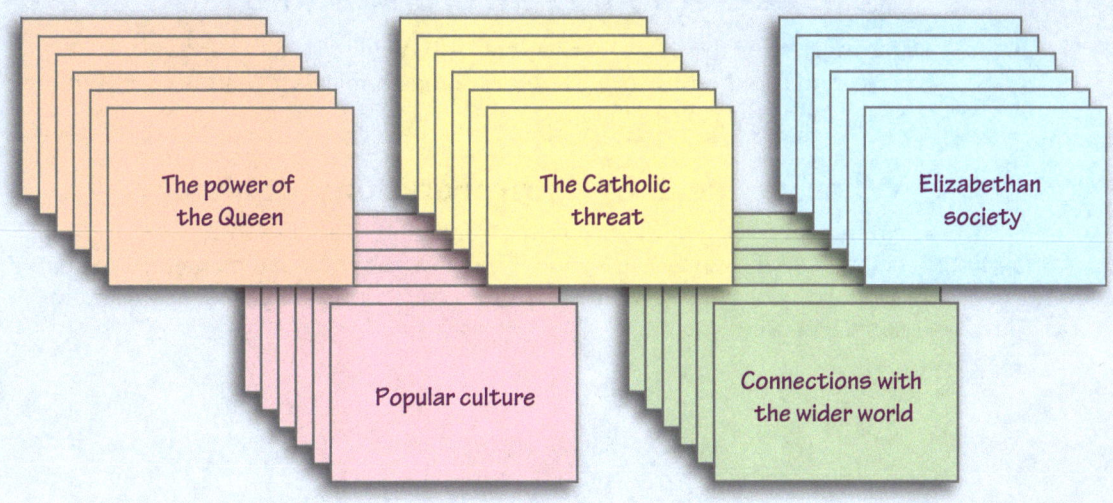

4. Podcasts

If you learn best by listening to information and explanations, you could record your knowledge and understanding by producing podcasts to summarise what you have learned about each of the five main issues. You could produce your podcast with a friend using a question and answer format.

You could produce a sixth podcast where you explain how each of the forces listed under 'Mind maps' on page 98 affected different aspects of Elizabethan life.

To be well-prepared for the examination you need revision notes that summarise the main points and provide detailed examples in a format that works best for you.

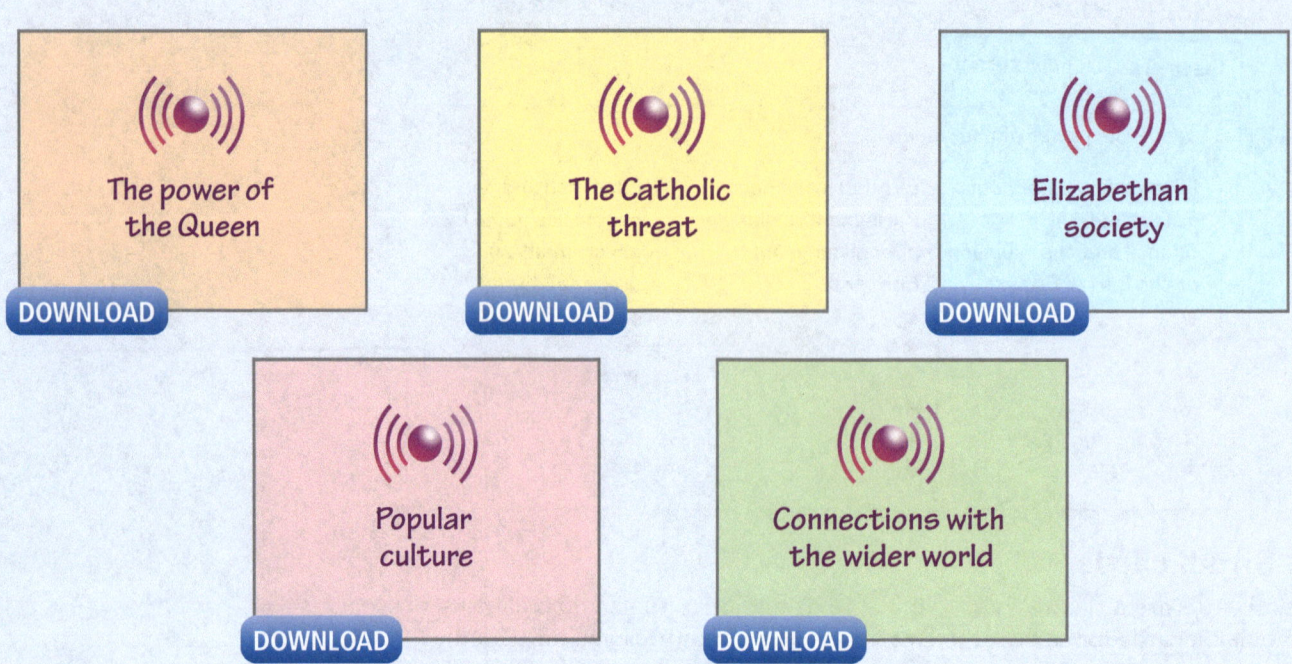

Understanding interpretations

To prepare for the examination, you will need to be clear about 'interpretations' of history. Here are some simple explanations and some suggestions for your revision.

What we mean by 'interpretations' of history

An interpretation of history is any version of events in the past that has been created at some later time. The interpretation can be made and shared by all sorts of people, in all sorts of ways, for all sorts of reasons. Here are some examples:

People or groups who create or advise on interpretations of the past	Ways in which interpretations may be shared	Reasons for creating interpretations of the past
Academics (professional historians, museum curators or archaeologists)	Non-fiction books	To educate or inform
	Fiction books	To entertain or amuse
	Websites	To persuade
Lecturers and teachers	Blogs	To commemorate
Writers and artists	Exhibitions and displays	
	Magazines	
Tourist organisations	Formal reports and articles	
	Plays	
Individuals or groups who are tracing the history of a family or an organisation	Films	
	Tourist information resources	
	Television/radio documentaries	
	Television dramas	
	Television light entertainment	
	Advertisements	
	Background to news reports	
	Drawings and paintings	
	Computer games	
	Theme parks	
	Souvenirs	
	Monuments	
	Ceremonies	

These tasks will help to sharpen your thinking about historical interpretations:

1. **Try to match up each of the people or groups in the left-hand column with the methods you think they might use to share their interpretations and the reasons why they have created them.**
2. **Look back through this book to find examples of historical interpretations. For each one that you find:**
   - briefly summarise what historical point it makes
   - list who created it, how it was shared with other people and what its purpose was.

How interpretations of the past may differ

People who look back on the past often disagree about what they find. They may disagree about all sorts of issues including:

- what actually happened and when
- whether an event or type of behaviour was 'typical' of the period in history when it happened
- why events or developments happened at all or why they happened at a certain time
- which person, factor or consequence was most significant and why
- how much change was happening, how quickly and how it affected different groups of people at the time
- what sources should be used and what they reveal
- what (if anything) we can learn from the events of the past.

Why interpretations of the past may differ

There are many different reasons why people offer different interpretations of the past. Here are a few suggestions:

- They may use different sources, for example someone working at a later date may be able to use newly discovered documents or new scientific techniques to throw more light on the issue.
- They may be faced with gaps in the evidence and may make different but reasonable guesses based on the sources they have.
- They use the same sources very carefully but honestly reach different conclusions.
- They are affected by their own background or context, for example the age in which they were working, their nationality, personality, beliefs and values may all affect their judgements.
- They may be creating their interpretation for different audiences, for example young children or foreign tourists rather than professional historians.
- They may be creating their interpretations for different reasons, for example to provide light-hearted entertainment rather than precise historical understanding.
- They may simply be less careful in applying good historical methods, for example failing to consider all available sources, misunderstanding what sources say, reaching conclusions that cannot be supported by the sources or failing to make their conclusions clear.

Look at the list you made of some historical interpretations that you found in this book (see page 101). Can you see any signs that any were affected by any of the influences listed above?

Preparing for the examination

Exam guidance

The depth study forms the second half of Paper 1: British History. It is worth twenty per cent of your GCSE. The whole exam lasts for 1 hour 45 minutes so you will have just over 50 minutes to answer the four questions on The Elizabethans.

Question 6a

You will be shown an interpretation of some aspect of Elizabethan history between 1580 and 1603. The interpretation may be in text form or an image. The question will start by explaining the point that the interpretation is making. You will have to show that you understand how it does this. The question will usually begin 'In Interpretation A the historian ... Identify and explain one way in which the historian does this.'

> **Example**
>
> 6 (a) In Interpretation A the illustrator portrays the wealth and comfort of an Elizabethan gentleman's house. Identify and explain one way in which the illustrator does this. (3 marks)
>
>
>
> Image from S. Purkis and J. Mason, *Tudor Gallery: A Sense of History, Primary*, p. 21, Addison Wesley Longman Ltd., London, 1997

Devise five questions like this using five different interpretations that you can find in this book. Try to use images with one or two and text with the others.

Question 6b

For this question you will be asked to suggest an area of further research into an aspect of the historical situation or issue that is the focus of question 6a. You will have to justify the suggestion you make. The question stem will usually be 'If you were asked to do further research on [Interpretation A], what would you choose to investigate? Explain how this would help us to analyse and understand [the topic in 6a].'

> 6 (b) If you were asked to do further research on one aspect of Interpretation A, what would you choose to investigate? Explain how this would help us to analyse and understand daily life in Elizabethan England. (5 marks)

For each of the questions you invented for 6a, write a brief 6b-style question.

Question 7

Question 7 requires you to explain how far and why two given interpretations differ. A typical stem is 'Interpretations B and C both focus on ... How far do they differ and what might explain any differences?'

Example

7 Interpretations B and C both focus on the power of Elizabeth I. How far do they differ and what might explain the difference? (12 marks)

Interpretation B – An extract from *The Making of the United Kingdom, 1500–1750*, a secondary school textbook written by J.F. Aylett in 1992.

Elizabeth I was England's only unmarried queen. Perhaps she knew that if she married an English nobleman, she would offend others. If she had married a foreigner she would not have been able to follow her own policies. And those policies were successful. When she died in 1603, England was one of the world's leading trading nations. It had also become a major power in Europe. Above all, she handed over a country that was more peaceful and united than ever before. Many people thought that she was wonderful. No wonder they looked back on her reign as a Golden Age.

Interpretation C – An extract from *A Brief History of Britain, 1485–1660*, written by the historian Ronald Hutton in 2010.

During her last years, her government was starting to show signs of strain. The Spanish war had reached stalemate, with the English more anxious to make peace than their opponents. Court politics had become unusually divisive and embittered, leading to the rebellion and execution of her final toy-boy, Essex, and then a monopoly of power by Burghley's son, Robert Cecil. The last Parliament of the reign turned directly upon the Queen over the issue of economic monopolies that she was granting as rewards to her followers; and she was forced to surrender to its demands. Her splendid costumes made an ever more glaring contrast with her physical decay: one Venetian ambassador reported that she stank so much it was wise to stand upwind of her.

Practise this type of question by using the example above.
Find differences in:

- what the two interpretations say
- what one interpretation includes that the other does not
- how the two interpretations are written, that is their style and tone.

Then try to explain why these differences might exist. You could use the list on page 102 to get you started but you should only use an idea from that list if you can back up your suggestion with good reasons to show that it might apply in this particular case.

Preparing for the examination

Question 8/9

You have a choice of two judgement questions. Question 8 or Question 9. These questions in the second part of Paper 1 are the most challenging. They ask you to make a judgement about a particular interpretation of an aspect of life in Elizabethan England, 1580–1603. You need to save enough time for this question because it is worth 20 marks.

Example

8   In his 2012 book, *The Watchers*, the historian Stephen Alford argued that the threat from Catholics created 'dangerous and uncertain times' in Elizabethan England. How far do you agree with this view?   (20 marks)

9   In his 1974 school textbook, *Tudors and Stuarts*, R.J. Unstead stated that Elizabethan adventurers 'successfully increased English trade in all parts of the world'. How far do you agree with this view?   (20 marks)

Depending on the interpretation given in the question, you may wish to agree completely, disagree completely or take a position where you can see some reasons for agreeing and some for disagreeing. You can get full marks for any of these types of answer provided that you:

- Show that you have understood exactly what the interpretation is claiming.
- Show that you understand any particularly important words, phrases or dates that the interpretation uses.
- Use very clear explanations and suitable, accurate supporting evidence to persuade the examiner that you are giving a very reasonable answer.
- Keep closely to the point all the way through your answer.

In the examples above, are there any words, phrases or dates in the interpretations that you would need to address in your answer?

Choose one of the example questions above and write a plan of how you would answer it. It is helpful to plan each paragraph in your answer so that it has a very definite main point that is clearly supported with accurate and appropriate evidence chosen from your knowledge of the period. Do this planning before you start to write in the exam.

Glossary

allotment small plot of land often used for growing vegetables

accession taking the throne as a king or queen

alms money or gifts such as food for the poor

almshouse a place made to house poor people

apprenticeship a period of training, usually seven years

armada large fleet of ships from Spain

artistic licence the right of writers, painters, poets, etc. to portray people and events in ways that are not strictly accurate

astrology study of stars to foretell the future

astronomy study of stars and planets

baiting provoking or attacking, e.g. bear-baiting

baptism the ceremony when a child or adult is accepted into the Christian church

Catholic a member of the Roman Catholic Church, led by the Pope

censorship preventing people from saying or publishing what they like

churchwarden person who helped the priest run a local church

colonisation taking land from people

colony land taken and ruled by a foreign power

commission pay someone to do or make something

contraception methods used to avoid becoming pregnant

court the large group of people who gathered around the queen wherever she was

courtier a member of the court

crucifix a cross with the figure of Jesus on it, popular with Catholics

culture way of life

cut-purse thief who stole goods by cutting the purse or bag from the owner's belt

economic to do with money

envoy person sent with a message or task

excommunicate expel from the Roman Catholic Church

exile a person sent to live far away, usually in a foreign country

faction small group, e.g. of courtiers

factory in Tudor times this was a trading base

familiar a demon in animal form kept by a witch, e.g. a cat

feminist a person who argues for women's rights in society

fertility ability of a person to have children or land to grow crops

gentry land-owning people in Tudor society, usually used to describe people who did not have titles

guild an organisation that organised crafts and trades such as carpenters or butchers

heir a person who inherits a title or property when anther dies

heretics unbelievers or people who accept false teachings. Elizabethan Catholics and Protestants accused each other of being heretics

hierarchy a system where people are organised in different layers of importance

house of correction place where poor people were put to work in Tudor times

husbandman a farmer

imp a small demon or wicked spirit

impotent weak, unable to look after yourself

interpretation a version or viewpoint

Jesuit a member of the Society of Jesus, an organisation of deeply committed Catholics

JP (Justice of the Peace) a person responsible for many aspects of local government in Tudor society

kinship family ties

laymen name given to people who are not priests

martyr someone who is prepared to die for his or her beliefs

Mass the most important Roman Catholic Church service

middling sort people in the middle of Tudor society, neither rich nor poor

misogyny dislike of and prejudice against women

monopoly the right in Tudor times to import and sell certain goods such as wine

navigation finding a route, e.g. at sea

nostalgic a love of the past or the 'good old days'

nuclear family parents and their children

ordain to make a person a priest

overseer of the poor person in a local church who had responsibility for looking after the poor in that area

pagan believing in many gods and spirits but not the Christian God

pageant a show

papist a name used by Protestants for Catholics, i.e. followers of the Pope

parish register the record of births, marriages and deaths in a local church

patriotic when a person loves his or her country very deeply

patronage system of providing employment and favours based on knowing people personally

pillage destroy

pillory wooden blocks that held prisoners by their head and hands

plunder steal

Poor Laws laws that set out how poor people were to be treated in Tudor times

poor relief a local tax to provide for the needs of the poor

Pope the leader of the Roman Catholic Church

poverty being poor

Presbyterianism a system of organising the church system where people choose who should be their leaders

privy private

privy chamber the Queen's personal rooms at court

privy council the small group of advisers closest to the Queen

probate inventory list of a person's belongings made after he or she died

propaganda spreading a one-sided message as widely as possibly

Protestant a Christian in western Europe who does not accept the leadership of the Pope

Puritan a particularly committed Protestant Christian

quarter sessions trials of local crimes held every three months by a JP

rack machine used to torture people by stretching their bodies

reconnaissance looking around

recusancy deliberate non-attendance at church in Elizabeth's time

recusants Catholics who refused to attend Protestant church services in Elizabeth's reign

rivet metal bolt or fastener

rogue dishonest person

rosary beads beads on a cord used by Catholics to help them pray

sabbat festival held by a meeting of witches

Sabbath a weekly holy day, e.g. Sunday for Christians

Secretary of State the Queen's leading adviser

secular not to do with the church

seminary a college where Catholic priests were trained

succession the arrangement of who should take over following the end of a king or queen's reign

successor person who takes over from another, e.g. as king or queen

supremacy being the most important, e.g. the Act of Supremacy said Elizabeth was the head of the English state and its church

traitor person who betrays his or her king, queen and country

treasonous an action that tries to betray or kill a king or queen

uniformity being the same, e.g. the Act of Uniformity made everyone worship the same way in Elizabeth's reign

vagabond same as vagrant

vagrant a poor person who roams around looking for work

yeoman a fairly wealthy farmer

Index

Accession Day 7, 20, 22, 23
Act Against Priests (1585) 30, 35
Act of Persuasions (1581) 30
Act Restraining Recusants (1593) 31
Act of Supremacy (1559) 28
Act of Uniformity (1559) 28
adventurers
    in America 84, 86–9
    in Asia 85, 90–5
alehouses 67
Allen, William 32, 33, 35
America, exploration and colonisation of 82, 84, 86–9
Anglo-Spanish War, 1585–1604 39–40
art 64
artistic licence 24
Asia, trade with 85, 90–5

Babington Plot, 1586 37
Ballard, John 37
Bankside, London 76
Blackadder II (TV series) 25
'Bloody Question' 35
Bond of Association 37
books 21
Burghley, Sir William Cecil, Lord 13, 14, 37

calendar customs 67, 68
Campion, Edmund 32, 33, 34, 35
Catholics
    decline of 27, 41
    English priests 32–5
    international affairs and 36–40
    laws and 28–31
    martyrs 26–7
Cecil, Robert 14, 15
Cecil, Sir William, Lord Burghley 13, 14, 37
censorship 21
children 52, 54
church papists 29
Clitherow, Margaret 31
Cobham family 52
colonisation, of America 86–9
conformers, Catholic 29
the court 9–13
courtiers 10, 12
craftsmen 48
culture 64–5
    magic and witches 70–3
    pastimes and festivities 66–9, 78–9
    theatres 74–7

Dee, Dr John 82
Devereux, Robert, Earl of Essex 14–15

Drake, Sir Francis 6–7, 39, 40, 83

East India Company 95
Eldred, John 91
Eliot, George 33, 34
Elizabeth (film) 25
Elizabeth I
    and calendar customs 68
    and Catholics 27, 28, 29, 31, 35
    death and funeral 96
    in film and on television 24–5
    and her court 9–15
    and her people 19–23
    images of 8, 21–2, 38
    and Mary, Queen of Scots 36, 37
    and Parliament 16–18
Elizabeth R (TV drama) 24
Essex, Robert Devereux, Earl of 14–15
exploration
    of America 84, 86–9
    Francis Drake 6, 83
    John Dee and 82
    trade with Asia 85, 90–5

family life 52–5
famine 57
feasts and feasting 46–7, 66
festivities 66–9, 78–9
films, Elizabeth I portrayed in 25
Fitch, Ralph 85, 91–2
food 46–7, 49, 51
food prices 57
football 67
Francis Drake 6–7, 39, 40, 83

gentry 9, 10, 46–7
Gilbert, Humphrey 84, 86
Golden Hind (ship) 6
'Golden Speech' Elizabeth I's, 1601 18, 21
government
    local 19
    Parliament 16–18
    patronage and the court 9–15
Grenville, Richard 88, 89
Guiana, South America 89

Harvington Hall, Worcestershire 43
Hilliard, Nicholas 64
historical interpretation 43, 100–2
houses 46, 48–9, 51, 60–1
husbandmen 48

India 90, 91–2

Jackson, Glenda 24

Jesuit priests 32, 35
Justices of the Peace (JPs) 19, 47, 59

Kapur, Shekhar 25
Kemp, Ursula 70
kinship 55

labourers 50–1, 56
ladies-in-waiting 12
Lambarde, William 19
Lancaster, James 85, 94–5
land ownership 47, 48, 50
Lane, Ralph 88, 89
laws, religious 28
Lee, Sir Henry 22
Leedes, William 91, 92
literature 64
local government 19
Lords Lieutenant 19

magic, belief in 71
marriage 53
Mary, Queen of Scots 7, 36–7
May Day 67, 78–9
middling people 48–9
Millais, John Everitt 80
miracle plays 74
monopolies 18
Montacute House 45, 46, 60–1
MPs (Members of Parliament) 16, 17, 18
Mughal Empire 91, 92
Munday, Anthony 33, 34
music 64

Newberry, John 91, 92
Newfoundland, North America 86
nobles 9, 10, 11, 47
North America, exploration and colonisation of 82, 84, 86–9

Owen, Nicholas (Little John) 42–3

parish feasts 66
Parliament 16–18
Parry, William 33
pastimes 66–9
patronage 9, 11, 17
Persons (Parsons), Robert 32, 33, 35, 37
Phelips, Sir Edward 46
Philip II of Spain 38, 39, 41
playhouses 21, 74–7
plays 21
plotters, Catholic 29
Poor Law (1601) 59
Pope Pius V 32
population growth 57

108

portraits, of Elizabeth I 8, 21–2, 38
poverty 50–1, 56–9
priests, Catholic 30, 32–5
priest's holes 33, 42, 43
printing presses 21
Privy Chamber 12
Privy Council 12, 16, 20, 21
probate inventories 48, 50
progresses, royal 20
propaganda 20–3, 35
Puritans
    in Parliament 17, 18
    and popular culture 68–9, 73, 77

Raleigh, Sir Walter 80–1, 84, 87, 89, 96
Recusancy Act (1587) 31
recusants 29, 30, 31
religion
    Catholics in Elizabethan times 26–41
    and Elizabeth I 23
    and popular culture 67, 68–9, 73, 77
    Puritan Parliamentary opposition 17, 18
Richardson, Miranda 25
Roanoke Island, North America 87, 88, 89
Roman Catholic faith see Catholics
Rowlande, Richard 35
Russell, Anne 10, 12

secretaries of state 13
seminary priests 32, 35
settled poor 56
Shakespeare, William 64, 74, 75
Sledd, Charles 33, 34
Spain 38–9
Spanish Armada, 1588 39–40
spice trade 90
sports 67
Story, James 91
Stubbs, John 17

television, Elizabeth I portrayed on 24–5
theatres 21, 74–7
Throckmorton Plot, 1583 37
Topcliffe, Richard 35
tradesmen 48
Tresham, Sir Thomas 28, 29, 30, 31, 33
Turkey Company 90, 91

unemployed poor 58–9
Unton, Sir Henry 44–5

vagabonds 58
vagrants 56, 58, 59
Victorians, impressions of Elizabethan times 79, 80, 97
Virginia, North America 81, 84, 88–9

Walsingham, Sir Francis 13, 33
Wentworth, Peter 18
Whitehall Palace, London 10
witches, persecution of 70–3

yeomen 48

Acknowledgements

The publishers would like to thank the following for permission to reproduce copyright material:

Photo credits: p.6 © Joel W. Rogers/Corbis; **p.7** © Bridgeman Images/TopFoto; **p.8** © Antiquarian Images/Mary Evans; **p.10** © TopFoto; **p.11** © Pictorial Press Ltd/Alamy Stock Photo; **p.12** *t* © World History Archive/Alamy Stock Photo; *b* © National Portrait Gallery, London; **p.13** *l* © World History Archive/Alamy Stock Photo; *r* © Print Collector/Hulton Archive/Getty Images; **p.14** © Granger Historical Picture Archve/Alamy Stock Photo; **p.15** © National Portrait Gallery, London; **p.16** © Unattributed photograph for Barnaby's Studios Ltd/Mary Evans Picture Library; **p.17** © Gillett, Frank (1874-1927)/Private Collection/The Stapleton Collection/Bridgeman Images; **p.18** © Look and Learn; **p.19** © National Portrait Gallery, London; **p.20** © Classic Image/Alamy Stock Photo; **p.21** *t* © The National Archives of the UK, ref. SP12/282 no.67 f.138; *m* © Nearby/Alamy Stock Photo; *b* © National Portrait Gallery, London; **p.22** © National Portrait Gallery, London; **p.23** © 1 Collection/Alamy Stock Photo; **p.24** © Moviestore collection Ltd/Alamy Stock Photo; **p.25** *t* © CBW/Alamy Stock Photo; *b* © AF archive/Alamy Stock Photo; **p.26** © Pollen (nee Baring), Daphne (1904-86) (after)/His Grace The Duke of Norfolk, Arundel Castle/Bridgeman Images; **p.28** © The Trustees of the British Museum; **p.30** © English School, (16th century)/By permission of the Governors of Stonyhurst College/Bridgeman Images; **p.31** © Flemish School, (16th century)/By permission of the Governors of Stonyhurst College/Bridgeman Images; **p.32** *l* © Reproduced by kind permission of the Syndics of Cambridge University Library; *r* © Mary Evans Picture Library/Alamy Stock Photo; **p.33** *t* © Michael Rhodes/TopFoto; *b* © World History Archive/Alamy Stock Photo; **p.34** © From The New York Public Library; **p.36** © Pictorial Press Ltd/Alamy Stock Photo; **p.37** © Print Collector/Hulton Fine Art Collection/Getty Images; **p.38** © Archivart/Alamy Stock Photo; **p.39** © World History Archive/Alamy Stock Photo; **p.43** *t* © Harvington Hall; *b* © Jon Lewis/Alamy Stock Photo; **pp.44–45** © National Portrait Gallery, London; **p.46** © Parliamentary Art Collection, WOA 2699; **p.47** © National Trust Images/Mike Thurstan; **p.48** © Lesley Pardoe/Alamy Stock Photo; **p.49** © Images of Birmingham; **p.50** © Edinburgh University Library; **p.51** © Weald & Downland Open Air Museum; **p.52** © Eileen Tweedy/Marquess of Bath/The Art Archive; **p.53** © Montacute House, Somerset, UK/National Trust Photographic Library/Nadia Mackenzie/Bridgeman Images; **p.54** © By kind permission of Viscount De L'Isle from his private collection at Penshurst Place, Kent, England; **p.55** © Mapseeker Publishing/Mary Evans Picture Library; **p.56** © 510 Collection/Alamy Stock Photo; **p.58** *t* © Fotosearch/Archive Photos/Getty Images; *b* © ullsteinbild/TopFoto; **p.59** © Francis Frith/Mary Evans Picture Library; **pp.60–61** © The National Trust Photolibrary/Alamy Stock Photo; **pp.62–63** A Fête at Bermondsey, c.1570 (oil on panel), Gheeraerts, Marcus, the Elder (c.1520–90) / Hatfield House, Hertfordshire, UK / Bridgeman Images; **p.64** *t* © Granger Historical Picture Archve/Alamy Stock Photo; *bl* © GL Archive/Alamy Stock Photo; *br* © Mark Fiennes/Bridgeman Images; **p.65** *t* © Flemish School, (17th century)/Fitzwilliam Museum, University of Cambridge, UK/Bridgeman Images; *m* © Art Directors & TRIP/Alamy Stock Photo; *b* © Look and Learn/Peter Jackson Collection/Bridgeman Images; **p.66** © Heritage Images/Hulton Archive/Getty Images; **p.69** © Flemish School, (17th century)/Fitzwilliam Museum, University of Cambridge, UK/Bridgeman Images; **p.70** © Art Directors & TRIP/Alamy Stock Photo; **p.71** *t* © Lambeth Palace Library, London, UK/Bridgeman Images; *b* © The British Library board, C.27.a.11, f.Ar; **p.73** © Lambeth Palace Library, London, UK/Bridgeman Images; **p.75** *t* © Lebrecht Music and Arts Photo Library/Alamy Stock Photo; *b* © Brenda Kean/123RF; **p.76** © Look and Learn/Peter Jackson Collection/Bridgeman Images; **p.78** © Bettmann/Getty Images; **p.79** © Robert Estall photo agency/Alamy Stock Photo; **p.80** © Classic Image/Alamy Stock Photo; **p.81** © Lebrecht Music and Arts Photo Library/Alamy Stock Photo; **p.82** *t* © World History Archive/Alamy Stock Photo; *b* © The British Library Board, C.21.e.12, title page; **p.83** © Look and Learn History Picture Library; **p.84** *t* © English School, (16th century)/Compton Castle, Torquay, Devon, UK/National Trust Photographic Library/Bridgeman Images; *b* © World History Archive/Alamy Stock Photo; **p.85** *t* © The National Library of Israel, Jerusalem; *b* © National Maritime Museum, Greenwich, London; **p.86** © English School, (16th century)/Compton Castle, Torquay, Devon, UK/National Trust Photographic Library/Bridgeman Images; **p.87** *t* © World History Archive/Alamy Stock Photo; *b* © The Art Archive/Alamy Stock Photo; **p.88** *l* © World History Archive/Alamy Stock Photo; *r* © The Trustees of the British Museum; **p.89** © Look and Learn History Picture Library; **p.90** © Dinodia Photos/Alamy Stock Photo; **p.91** © The National Library of Israel, Jerusalem; **p.92** © Pictures from History/Bridgeman Images; **p.93** © Mughal School, (16th century)/Victoria & Albert Museum, London, UK/The Stapleton Collection/Bridgeman Images; **p.94** © National Maritime Museum, Greenwich, London; **p.95** © Classic Image/Alamy Stock Photo; **p.96** © British Library/Robana/REX/Shutterstock; **p.97** *t* © British Library/Robana/REX/Shutterstock; *b* © Peter Macdiarmid/Getty Images News.